Raising Your Money-Savvy Family for Next Generation Financial Independence

By Carol Pittner and Doug Nordman

Foreword by JL Collins,
international best-selling author
of *The Simple Path To Wealth*

ISBN: 978-1-7350661-1-0 (Paperback)
ISBN: 978-1-7350661-2-7 (Hardcover)

Library of Congress Control Number: 2020938511

Front cover image and Book Design by Giada Mannino

Printed by Choose FI Media, Inc. in the United States of America.

First printing edition 2020.

Choose FI Media, Inc.
P.O. Box 3982
Glen Allen, VA 23058

www.choosefi.com
childFIRE.com

Carol

To My Spouse: Always... just five seconds behind the other.

To My Parents: Thank you for guiding me into adulthood.
I know I made that process way harder than it needed to be!

To Our Kid(s): We love you very much!

To The FI Community: Keep talking, writing, teaching, and learning. You've been an incredible source of inspiration to the Pittner-Nordman family.

Doug

To My Spouse: For once again saying "Nords, you need to write this book" while knowing full well that you'd end up editing it. And editing it again. And just once more.

To My Daughter: It's my second book, and you're still teaching me about writing. This one's even better!

To My Son-In-Law: For getting to know his in-laws and for marrying into this family anyway. (It must be love!) I hope our grandparenting is as good as your parenting.

To The CampFI Alumni: For asking the questions... and for proofreading our answers.

Contents

Foreword

by JL Collins, author of *The Simple Path To Wealth*

I should have written this book.

Along with my daughter Jessica, of course.

This less-than-noble thought, I admit, was my first when Doug told me he was writing *Raising Your Money-Savvy Family* with his daughter Carol.

This is, after all, a brilliant concept and with the alternating sections between Doug and Carol, a brilliant execution.

Carol and Jessica are almost precisely the same age. Plus, I knew there was a need for such a book. I had watched Jessica give talks to FI (financial independence) groups about growing up with me as her father.

These talks didn't attract just parents with small children as I initially expected. They attracted parents with children of all ages, including those now adults themselves. They attracted grandparents and those hoping to be. They attracted young couples and singles with no kids in their lives...at least not yet.

In short, these talks were attended by anyone who has kids, had kids, might have kids, or who has kids who have kids or who might have kids. Even those of us who used to be kids and just wonder what our parents could have done better in this financial education task.

And that, if you've lost track or weren't keeping score, is just about everyone.

Raising money-savvy children is not only a topic of keen interest to a wide range of people, it is critical information they need. Information you need.

But once I had the manuscript in hand and began to read, I realized I couldn't have written this book.

For one, Doug was simply much better at teaching these financially savvy lessons to his daughter than I was to mine. After all, those talks my daughter gives? Those are mostly about what I did wrong and how we (finally!) got past my blunders.

Doug and Carol, on the other hand, lay out in this book a series of steps, techniques, and approaches that actually work for both parent and child. Together they take you on their journey from her earliest childhood years to grammar school, to high school, to college, to her young adult life.

At each step I found myself muttering, "Now that's a cool idea. Wish I'd thought of that. Man, where was this book 25 years ago!?"

This is a very practical guide.

When, you might wonder, should you begin teaching your kids about money? When they stop trying to eat it.

Choking on a quarter shouldn't be the first lesson. Although it makes for pretty dramatic reading. Turns out, you should wait until you can safely leave them alone with coins.

But once they stop putting the coins in their mouths, those little round metal discs become great counting and learning tools. One memorable lesson Carol shares: Coins are easy to lose.

If that sounds simple, it is no less profound in the lesson it teaches a child. Coins, and by extension money itself, are indeed easy to lose.

It is a short step from there to teaching children that money can be exchanged for things and how that process is best handled; how buying decisions have consequences, some good and others not so much; how those precious coins are gone forever once they are spent. For better or worse, left in their place is your purchase.

Children will, of course, make mistakes in their spending. That's the point, and the benefit. Never again will it be safer or less damaging to make such mistakes than with little at risk and under your watchful parental eye.

A mistake can be a simple and profound lesson which gives children a tangible measure of worth to apply against what they chose to buy.

Another important lesson, and one I certainly wish I'd had back in the day: That "watchful parental eye" needs to be a non-judgmental eye as well. Children need to make these mistakes and to learn from them on their own.

Letting them have their own learning experience trumps your lectures.

We gave our daughter an allowance, and it worked out OK. It would have worked out better had I read Chapter 3 in this book: *Managing Allowances, Chores, and Jobs.* Understanding the difference between Chores and Jobs alone is worth the price of admission.

As is the concept of "The Kid 401(k)"—another stroke of brilliance I wish I had thought of, or at least read about.

With each of these concepts, and the many others covered in this book, we get to read the differing perspectives between parent and child. It is especially fascinating to hear Carol describe how she saw these things as a child and her often amusing insights into them now as an adult.

These early constructs lead to a far easier transition into the real world of checking accounts, ATMs, debit cards, IRAs, employer investment accounts, savings rates, stocks, index funds, shopping, credit cards, taxes, cars, and the value of financial independence.

We get to travel with Carol (and Doug!) as she grows in age, understanding, and responsibility. We get to join her on her sometimes difficult, complex, and ultimately successful road into adult life.

Reflecting back over these pages as I write this foreword, we did many of the same things as Doug and Carol. Lessons on investing, savings, spending. But they did them better, more completely, and with more thought. Those are profound differences.

Today, as the father of an adult daughter myself, I can especially relate to Doug's discussion of his transition from parent to coach.

Page by page, you can't help but be impressed by the creativity and financial savvy the Nordmans brought not just to guiding Carol to a financially sound outlook, but to their lives together in general.

It is not just about money. It is about living an inspired, fulfilling, and free life. It is about learning to own your time.

As Carol says at the end...

"Most importantly, we get to spend more time together, and that's something we find priceless."

No, I shouldn't have, couldn't have, written this book. But I sure wish it had been around when I was raising Jessica. Of course, then she wouldn't have all that material for her talks.

JL Collins

Financial Independence Gives You Choices

> **"**
>
> IT'S NOT ABOUT BEING RICHER THAN THE RICHEST, OR BANKRUPT-PROOF. IT'S ABOUT HAVING ENOUGH MONEY TO HAVE THE POWER OF CHOICE, AND FIND JOY, AND LIVE THE LIFESTYLE THAT TRULY MAKES YOU HAPPY, NO MATTER WHAT HAPPENS IN LIFE.
>
> MARGE NORDMAN
> FINANCIALLY INDEPENDENT SINCE 1999

DOUG
"How Will Your Daughter Reach Financial Independence?"

Welcome to our stories!

In 1992, Marge and I were overwhelmed after starting our family. Our daughter Carol was full of energy and curious about everything. Whatever we were doing, she wanted to know more about it. When Carol started asking questions about money, we parents showed her how we used ours. As Marge and I approached our financial independence, we continued teaching Carol how to manage her money.

In 2014, after Carol graduated from college and started her own career, Marge and I began attending CampFI meetups with other people who were pursuing their financial independence. At one meetup, I gave a talk about investing for FI. A parent in the audience hijacked my train of thought by asking: "I understand how you reached FI, and you've talked about your daughter. How will she reach FI?"

I was stumped. I'd written about the cost of raising a family and about starting a teenager's Roth IRA, but I'd never put it all together into "raising a money-savvy family." Our young adult seemed to be off to a good start, but it was too early to tell whether she was even interested in FI.

I blathered an answer about giving our young kid an allowance to learn how to make choices and manage her money. The parent nodded politely and we moved on to other questions.

About a year later, I met the same parent and asked how their kids were doing with money. The answer was "Well, I tried giving them an allowance, but I felt they were wasting it and I gave up. We'll try again when they're older."

Another year later, I gave another talk at a CampFI. The very first question was from a parent of a large family: "How do we raise our kids for FI?" At least this time I had a better answer, but we still agreed that kids had to make a lot of mistakes along the way.

When I told Marge about answering the same question for a second time, she said: "Nords, you need to write that book."

After that financial meetup, we visited Carol and her spouse for a few weeks. One evening around the dinner table we mentioned the money-savvy family question and asked "grownup Carol" what she had thought of our plans when she was "growing-up Carol."

> **"**
> ## HOW DO WE RAISE OUR KIDS FOR FI?

To my surprise and delight, Carol lit up the room with her memories. We reminisced about all the tactics we'd tried with her, and what worked. We parents had good resources for some of our techniques, and we'll share them here.

We also talked about what didn't work. Back then, as Carol grew older (and more curious), Marge and I wandered way off the beaten trail of the library's parenting books. We brainstormed more parenting ideas between us and then tried to implement those plans with Carol, but the results weren't always what we expected.

By the end of dinner, Carol and I decided to write this book together. As the family discussion rambled on through dessert, I took notes and we put together an outline.

Marge proposed that Carol and I write alternating sections: our "brilliant" parenting ideas contrasted with Carol's perceptions of how they really worked out. We want you to see both sides of our stories before you try these financial tactics with your family.

CAROL
Raising Your Money-Savvy Family, The Next Generation

That night around the dinner table with my parents and my husband K.J. (in 2018) sparked many memories of how I learned to manage my money. Some memories were happy, like the beloved pencil vending machine in elementary school that ate up the majority of my kindergarten allowance (those were some really cool pencils!). Other memories were somber, like the mood of my high school as the Great Recession took its toll on certain friends, classmates, and teachers.

There was one memory that came to the forefront, as it always did whenever the topic of my financial education came up. It was the time Mom sat me down (for what reason, I no longer remember), and uttered the quote that opens this book. I didn't know what "financial independence" was at the time, but I did understand the "privilege of choice," and how managing money led to more and more positive choices in life. It's that power of choice that drives my husband and me to continue managing our money well.

By pure coincidence, a few days after that dinner our money enabled a major life choice. With K.J. 's encouragement and another look at our finances, I decided to leave Active Duty (full-time) work in the U.S. Navy and move to the Reserves (part-time) work. The move would be a major cut to my salary and I would lose most of my benefits. But the move meant I could be a stay-at-home mom, and be there for our future kids. It also meant I could try writing, both as a hobby and maybe as a small source of income. Because K.J. and I had been saving so much over the previous five years, the choice to work was because it's "what we wanted to do," not "what our finances will let us do."

Just over seven months later, and exactly two weeks after my last day on my ship, K.J. and I found out I was pregnant. And as I write this introduction from the comfort of my living room couch, our firstborn is fast asleep in her portable crib next to me.

I can't wait until I can start teaching our daughter about how to reach her own financial independence.

DOUG
Teach Your Kids To Manage The Money You're Spending To Raise Them

Where do you find the money to teach your kids how to manage their money?

As we describe the ways that we taught our daughter to manage her money, you'll notice that raising her cost...a lot of money. It was cheap when she was younger, but the numbers got bigger as she got older. You may be wondering where that came from—a hidden trust fund? Bitcoin? Warren Buffett?

I wish we'd had those resources. Frankly, my most valuable resource was my determination to do a better job of teaching Carol about financial literacy than my parents had done with me.

Marge and I started our military careers in 1982. We married in 1986, and in 1999 we reached financial independence on our high savings rate. I retired in 2002. Marge left active duty in 2001 for a part-time career in the Reserves and then retired in 2008. Our life is very good.

More importantly, we've shown that our financial independence is sustainable. I'm the author of a book about U.S. military personal finance, and I've blogged about it at The Military Guide for over a decade. Today we know that our money will last longer than we will. You can read more about that in Appendix B at the back of this book.

When Marge and I started our family, we were motivated to get our financial act together. We made smart choices about reducing our (wasted) spending and earning more income. We enjoyed the challenge of living a frugal yet fulfilling life, and we avoided deprivation. When we cut our expenses, we invested the savings.

We showed Carol how to do the same things. She made plenty of money mistakes while she was younger, and she learned from her errors. Instead of Marge and me giving more of our money to Carol, we gradually gave her more control over the part of our budget for raising her. The money would have been spent on her either way, and by her teen years she was making her own smart choices.

You're reading the result of our family collaboration. I'm thrilled to be working with my adult daughter in the driver's seat, and I'm enjoying the ride.

SUMMARY
How To Use This Book

The lawyers make us say it: Carol and Doug are not child psychologists, family coaches, or certified financial advisors.

However we know quite a bit about saving and investing for financial independence.

We're sharing our stories to inform and entertain you as you raise your family. We're simply frugal parents in two different generations who achieved (and will achieve) our financial independence by aligning our spending with our values. We'll explain what worked for us—and what didn't work.

Marge and Doug's parenting experience has boosted the success of a young adult, and we think that our techniques will work for you too. Carol and Doug have written our family's memoir to help you find your parenting path. We'll offer suggestions that you can adapt to your situation, yet this is not a manual of how things must be done.

We've organized our advice in chronological order, but every family is different. The chapter titles describe goals or schools, not specific ages. Don't worry about a date or an age, and please don't compare your kid's progress to other kids. Children need to learn to measure their progress against their internal standards. You're there to show them how you did it for yourself, and how they can do it on their own.

We'll start each chapter with a summary of its financial terms and concepts, and we'll end each chapter with a checklist of goals to consider pursuing in your family.

As a parent, it's important for you to focus on their developing cerebral cortex and to help them be aware of their money emotions. They're going to make plenty of money mistakes before their brains can analyze adult choices. You're there to let them fail safely while avoiding serious damage. You want to help them survive their mistakes in the security of home and family instead of after high school or (even worse) when they're at their first adult job.

We'll help you develop your techniques. You'll help your kids understand their feelings and their choices, and then you'll help them talk through a better plan for the next time.

To paraphrase George S. Patton, a famous WWII American general: *"Don't tell your kids how to manage their money. Tell them what needs to be done with it, and let them surprise you with their creativity."*[1]

Marge and Doug made plenty of mistakes along the way, and we'll describe them in this book. However, our high savings rate overcame all of those mistakes. We knew about the math of compound growth, but even today we're still surprised by its power. If you've never heard of the financial independence movement or its math, then you can read more about that in Appendix B at the back of the book.

We're not going to tell you how to invest your money. (The world-famous author who wrote the foreword has already written about that!) We'll show you how to exploit a high savings rate and compound growth to create your own next-generation financial independence. We'll show you how we taught our daughter these lessons as well. You already know what needs to be done, and you'll surprise yourself with your ingenuity at making it happen.

Read on, and we'll share a few of our surprises.

---

[1] "George S. Patton Quotes." BrainyQuote.com. BrainyMedia Inc. Accessed January 25, 2020. https://www.brainyquote.com/quotes/george_s_patton_159766

CHAPTER ONE

The Big Picture On Raising A Money-Savvy Family

> **"**
>
> THINK OF YOURSELF AS A CURATOR RATHER THAN A CONSUMER.
>
> **CHRISTINE KOH**
> AUTHOR OF *MINIMALIST PARENTING*

> **FINANCIAL TERMS AND CONCEPTS**
> **IN THIS CHAPTER**
>
> - Cost estimates of raising a family.
> - A $20 bill seems less valuable to today's kids than to their parents as kids.
> - Emphasize managing money rather than building wealth.
> - The "5Ws and How" applied to teaching kids about money
> - The education fund grows bigger when it has more years to compound.
> - Financial management in just 20 minutes a day.

DOUG
The Cost Of Raising A Family

In 2017, the U.S. Department of Agriculture estimated the cost of raising a child at over $233,000.[2] The USDA's "average expenses" give more insight about America's hyper-consumer lifestyle than the true cost of feeding a few more mouths at the table.[3] As Ms. Koh notes in the epigraph above, you can curate your family life instead of being a consumer.

I dug into our family financial archives and determined that we'd spent just under $156,000. That includes academic tutoring and a

---

[2] You can see a breakdown of the categories and run your own calculations at the USDA's website. We've linked to it in the "Resources" section at the end of the book.

[3] See "USDA Food Cost Data from 1993" in Dacyczyn 1999, pp. 588–611.

couple of expensive sports, as well as living in a high cost-of-living area. With today's resources for reaching financial independence, you could raise your first child with a lot less. Your kids might not have everything they wanted but they'll have everything they need to launch into an independent life.

Raising a family might even improve your finances.

It's reassuring to learn that the expense of child rearing is a very wide bell curve with fat tails, and it's a relief to know that you can do it for even less money than we spent. But if you spent "only" $156K to launch your first child from the nest, then how can this possibly boost your net worth?

Yeah, I know, some of you experienced parents are snickering: *"Because you won't have any spare time in your life to spend more money on anything else!"* I can't argue with that. Raising our daughter involved far more trips to the park and the library than to Europe.

The hidden benefit of raising a family is that it forces new parents to start adulting. In my teens and twenties, I needed every bit of the structure and discipline that the military could provide. My spouse and I were already frugal and she taught me how to invest, but I had a lot to learn about the finances of raising a kid. When we turned our study into a nursery, we encountered an overwhelming logistics challenge of stocking it with baby gear. Of course our frugal skills eventually took care of that list with thrift stores and garage sales.

But we parents didn't just trade our travel budget for a pile of diapers. Nearly every new parent has experienced this sentiment after labor and delivery: "Holy cow, we're responsible for a new human. We'd better grow up and get our act together!" Starting a family makes you get a handle on your life.

You behave more responsibly. Admittedly you're also too tired to get into as much trouble as you used to. Nothing improves your driving more than strapping a baby seat into the vehicle. Racy sports cars are replaced by larger, safer kid-haulers. You spend less on high-end furniture and appliances and you focus on baby-proofing. You'll still visit the emergency room on a weekend, but this time you're worrying about your baby's cough or an ear infection instead of wild partying or picking up a co-worker after a night of too much fun. For at least the next 18 years, you have to set a well-behaved example for a new little person who will imitate everything you say and do.

Before you have kids, you might not want to examine the details of your budget. Once you have kids, however, you're tracking your spending just to figure out where it's all going.

Better yet, you start planning for everyone's future. It's not just getting the kids over to the park to burn off some energy before nap time. You not only take fewer risks with your life, but you cut back on risky behavior with your money. You continue saving and investing, and you're more thoughtful with your career planning. You might still change jobs or even start your own business, but you'll be much more analytical about the decision—and you'll work a lot harder to make it pay off.

I'd like to think that my spouse and I would have saved for financial independence with or without starting a family. However, starting a family made our goals much more compelling, and our daughter motivated us every day. Our planning for financial independence changed from a fantasy to a reality. I wanted to spend less time working and more time helping my daughter grow up.

Don't let the USDA scare you about starting a family. Instead, you can handle your family budget in the same way that you do for financial independence: track your expenses and then spend the money only where you find the most value. Before long you'll have your expenses in line with your priorities, you'll be saving far more, and you'll be on your personal path to financial independence.

CAROL
Learning Takes Time

I've always believed that young kids should learn about money, partly because I learned about money as a kid, and partly because I screwed up money often enough as a kid that I needed extra time to practice; the kind of time that adults don't have with all the other responsibilities and distractions that come with adulting.

In many ways, using money is an integral part of everyday life, just like practicing personal hygiene or communicating with other people. Why can't kids start learning about money while they're still kids? What's so complicated or special about money that kids must, well, become adults first?

WHAT'S SO COMPLICATED OR SPECIAL ABOUT MONEY THAT KIDS MUST, WELL, BECOME ADULTS FIRST?

Money is not complicated. Any kid can learn about it.

When I became a parent myself, I questioned when I should start teaching my kid about...everything, really. When do I start teaching her how to brush her teeth? Probably when she has teeth and the ability to hold things like a toothbrush. When do I teach her not to run into the street? Probably around the time she figures out how to walk. When do I start teaching her about money? Same idea: as soon as she starts interacting with money, or observing interactions with money.

So if your kids have seen money, or watched interactions with money, then it's time to teach them about money before they get in "adult-serious" trouble with it. The last thing you want is your kid run over by a debt truck as they run into the middle of Spending Street!

DOUG
Teaching Your Kids To Manage Money, Not Just Save It

While you're modeling money-savvy behavior for your family, you're also teaching your kids to manage their own money for their futures.

By "manage," I mean that they're learning how to use it. They practice by counting coins, storing cash in a wallet or purse, and buying ice cream. Eventually they'll learn how to save it, but when they're younger they have to get comfortable with spending it first. The point of this tutoring is education, not accumulating wealth.

Along the way we parents have to learn a few skills too, and the first one is appreciating the generational differences.

When we were kids, $20 was a lot of money. Now that we're adults, $20 buys a lot less than it used to. Although we parents are keenly aware that our money buys less, we still have our childhood emotional reactions at the sight of a $20 bill.

Yet to our kids, that $20 is nowhere near as valuable as we remember.

Once you've had a few emotional reactions to your kid's money behavior, you can appreciate how they feel while they're learning how to manage their money. You'll teach them how to deal with their feelings, and how to manage ever-larger amounts as they grow older.

Here's the tough part for parents: kids only learn fiscal responsibility through several episodes of fiscal irresponsibility.

We learned about these concepts from David Owen's book *First National Bank Of Dad* (look for it in your local library). He says that young children want to learn how to handle money, **but parents have to be willing to live with their kid's mistakes.**

The learning starts as soon as they get their hands on it. When Grandma sends $20 to her precocious grandchild for their birthday or Christmas, your kid knows that money is a powerful tool. They've watched their parents use money, and they've seen other kids use it on TV. Now they have the power!

This is a "teachable moment." If a parent tries to convince the kid to save their money instead of using it, then the child's financial motives are not aligned with the parents'. To a six-year-old, it makes no sense to put their money in some mysterious scheme called "the college fund." You're trying to force the concept of deferred gratification on someone who's still developing the mental and emotional capacity to even understand the vocabulary.

From their perspective, college is two more lifetimes away! You're asking them to surrender their hard-earned assets (er, I mean, Grandma's gift) to some faceless financial institution where it's apparently locked away forever. Then you're telling them how good it'll feel when they finally recover "their" money from lockup and get to use it.

This concept is so prevalent in every child's life that even Walt Disney Studios' Mary Poppins movies frequently discuss money.

If parents force kids to save their money, then clearly a kid's only rational reaction is to spend it before those crazy grownups try to confiscate it. Forced savings can inadvertently teach young kids to spend everything they get before they lose it. The harder you try to be an authority figure in this debate, the longer your kids resist the tyranny.

Resolve this conflict by avoiding it. Apply your parental jiu-jitsu and let your kids take over.

Use Grandma's teachable moment to help your kids learn how to use this powerful new tool. Be a friendly financial advisor, not a dictator. Share their joy when they come into a pile of cash! Begin building trust by helping them keep their money in a safe place, and then start a discussion about how they'll use it. What will they do with it? What could they spend it on? Do they know how much something costs? How many dollar bills are in twenty dollars? How will they feel when it's all spent on toys and candy? How could they get more of it?

When they (inevitably) waste Grandma's gift and run out of money, sympathize with them and validate their feelings. (They'll go through this cycle more than once.) Show them how to avoid running out of money, and model the correct behavior in your own financial life. As they master the basics of money management then you can help them with bigger and more powerful concepts.

Help your kids learn financial responsibility by allowing them to be irresponsible, and then guide them to explore and understand how that makes them feel.

Eventually they'll figure out spending and saving, but it might take them until middle school. Until then, parents can think of their kids running around the yard lighting $20 bills on fire like Fourth of July sparklers. It's a thrill while it lasts, but it's quickly used up. Get used to seeing it. Remind them of their choices, but let them scorch their fingers.

As a parent, you're ready to advise them **only** when they're ready to learn. You want to help them develop their money skills, not just dump a bunch of rules on them. Kids learn by trial and error (lots of errors!) and you want them to make those errors at home. *You want them to learn their money skills in a safe and loving environment where they can make mistakes*, instead of when they're in college with new roommates and a student loan counselor.

After they burn through a few gifts they'll realize that they're tired of being poor. Once they understand that they're in charge of managing their money, they're ready to learn how to earn it and save it for their future.

Then they're ready to turn those feelings of "no money" into "building wealth."

CAROL
Mirror, Mirror, On The Wall... Do I Have To Listen?

As a kid, you don't get a lot of choices in life. You don't get to choose your parents, your (lack of) siblings, your abode, your hometown, your family history, or any other aspect of your lot in life. But also as a kid, you do get a single and super-important choice every single day; if you're lucky, you even get this one choice multiple times in a day. That choice is: do I listen to my parents-guardians-authority figures who are in charge of me?

As those authority figure(s), many things will be done to get kids to listen. Deals and bets will be made, a little begging may occur, and maybe a few dirty tricks will be played here and there. But no matter how much parents try to coerce or discipline or manipulate or control their kids, it's ultimately on the kids to decide whether or not they want to listen to their parents.

Additionally, kids are very observant little monste—I mean, creatures that watch every little thing that parents do. Just when the parents think they've successfully hidden away from their kids in a pantry, a little set of eyes appears at the crack in the door, reminding you that those kids still see everything you do.

And the same extends to money. Kids see it when their parents are wearing their wealth instead of saving it. Kids see it when their parents are buying extensive renovations for the house instead of saving for the future. Kids know when parents spend late nights with their heads in their hands, trying to figure out how to overcome a pit of debt. Kids recognize when parents are telling the kids to "do as I say, not as I do." And kids, bless their hearts, don't hesitate to call out their parents about it.

So when it comes to building good money habits in your kids, take a look in your own mirror on the wall. Are you telling your kids to follow money principles that you don't follow yourself? Are you providing an example to follow in their own future?

At the same time, no family is perfect. You may invest all of your time and money in your kids, who decide not to listen to you...for a while. Or you may find out that your kids are better at handling money than you. Either way, it's better to start than it is to wait when it comes to teaching your kids about money.

So regardless of your habits as parents, and regardless of who your kids are, where do we start? How do you know when your child is ready to learn your money lessons? When will teachable moments be "age appropriate?" Each child is different, so saying "do this step at this age" won't do anyone any good.

What I offer instead is a general concept that looks a lot like the journalism concept called "the 5Ws and How," only applied to teaching your kids about money. It's a concept partially dictated by your eagerness to teach your child, and partially dictated by your child's level of maturity. Each part of the concept is as follows:

WHO: think of "who's who in the zoo," the stage where a kid learns to recognize different kinds of coins and bills, learns how to count money, and forms positive experiences with money, just as a kid learns how to recognize other "whos" like parents, siblings, other relatives, and authority figures like police, teachers, and even Mom and Dad's bosses. If kids are pointing out cats and dogs and swings and cars, they're ready to learn about different kinds of coins, as well as what paper money is.

WHAT: the stage where a kid decides what to spend their money on (or not); where kids learn the difference between wants and needs. This stage will result in a lot of mistakes, regrets, lessons learned, and eventually will become "experience." This stage often doesn't have an ending and lasts well into adulthood. And this stage cannot start until kids have some money of their own that they get to decide on. It has to be the kid's money, not "Mommy and Daddy's money," and it can answer a kid's question of "WHAT do you want?"

WHEN: the stage where a kid decides when to (not) use their money; where kids learn about time-dependent concepts like compounding interest and certificates and return on investment (ROI). Another stage where there's no ending, but again, to start this stage, kids need some money of their own. Kids also need to grasp the concept of "long term," meaning anything from months to years to decades of time.

WHERE: the stage where a young adult decides where their money goes; said another way, this is where kids start bridging the concepts of saving, spending, and investing, and make real decisions on what to do with their money in the longer term, such as opening specific bank accounts, investing in the stock market, choosing investment categories like gold or cryptocurrency or stocks (both tangible and intangible), or other means of asset allocations. This is where kids go beyond the general concept of "learning how to manage money" and into the advanced concept of "maximizing savings while minimizing maintenance costs." This stage will happen at different ages for different kids, and may be as early as middle school if they're interested in investing.

WHY: the stage where a maturing investor (formerly a kid) ties all their knowledge up into personal goals, and determines the purpose for their money. Will it fund a new cell phone or an expensive school trip? This stage covers both short- and long-term goals, and one possible end goal is financial independence (FI), achieved during adulthood.

HOW: the stage repeated and re-evaluated again and again in your child's adult life; where a mature adult decides how to achieve their WHY using the skills developed in the WHO, WHAT, WHEN, and WHERE stages. This is where an adult will decide how to produce income (a paid salary, starting their own business, flipping investment rental properties, and so on) and then how to sustain a comfortable lifestyle on that income.

You may find that some stages overlap or go out-of-order for your child. For example, some kids will remember that the ice cream truck comes by every Tuesday at 2:00pm (WHEN), and then grasp that they should save up their money for ice cream (WHAT) on Tuesdays. And that's ok. As long as you feel like a concept is educational—and not overwhelming or negative—for your child, keep using it.

As for teaching the HOW stage, that will slowly come about as a child grows up and develops tastes and personality. Parents will notice what interests their kids and what doesn't, and the teachable moments will become apparent from there.

DOUG
Start Saving Now For Your Child's Education

Begin with the end in mind: the education savings fund for when your progeny launches from the nest.

Yeah, I know. You've barely gone through the first pallet of diapers and we're already yammering about college funds. You don't even know if they want to go to college.

No worries. We're bringing it up now because it's a lot easier (and cheaper) when you start early. We're raising the subject right after birth because it gives you plenty of time to turn your plan into action. Someday your child will be a young adult and managing their education fund, whether it's for trade school or college or an MBA. For now, it's your job to make sure there's going to be a fund to manage. It's a long-term project which parents can tackle while their kid is still in diapers.

The earlier you start your savings, the more time your investments will have to grow. Compound interest is a wonderful part of the math for your kid's education (and your financial independence), but it needs time to work.

Your personal experience will guide your savings. Maybe you feel no obligation to fund your kid's college education because of your own background, and if you have a large family then everyone has to share limited financial resources. Or maybe you want to make the parenting sacrifice to save enough for four years at a private university.

We don't know what education after high school will look like in 15 years, and perhaps your kids won't even want to go to a physical university campus. There's a huge financial gap between taking online classes and getting into Harvard for desk-and-chalkboard lectures. The important parenting point is to start building that education fund as soon as you can.

The size of that fund is your personal choice, and it depends on your values as well as your savings rate. More importantly, you have to save for your own retirement before you save for someone else's education. We've heard it before: *"Your child can get scholarships and student loans for their education, but there are no scholarships or loans for your retirement."* Take care of your retirement security before you sacrifice for their education. (Your kids would want you to do this too, because they don't want to have to support you in your old age.) Maybe your goal is saving enough now to compound into an amount which will pay for two years at the local community college.

Marge and I built a great education fund, and in Chapter 8 we'll discuss what else you can do with it when your young adult forges their own path.

Whatever education goal you choose to support, it's a lot easier to start saving a few hundred dollars a month when they're babies than it will be to save a thousand dollars a month during their teens. When your kids open their birthday and holiday gifts, you'll have to find your own way to set aside the money for their education. Grandma's cash will help them learn how to manage their money now, but for the first 18 years you'll have to manage the education fund on your own.

We're not going to belabor the details of building the education fund or receiving financial aid, but the 529 college savings plan (in the United States) is the easiest place for most of it. A 529 account offers tax-deferred compounding, and grandparents can contribute too! You control how much you save, what assets you invest in, and your expense ratios of the investments you buy.

Read through the advice at websites like SavingForCollege.com and see whether your state provides a tax break, but you can start your 529 with any state. 529s were created in 1996, when Carol was already four years old, and we started using one soon after that.

Start investing aggressively in passively-managed total stock market index funds with low expense ratios, and plan to contribute to those funds for at least 10 years. Their long-term growth will compound faster than inflation until your kid is about 13 years old, and then you'll gradually shift to a conservative asset allocation of short-term bond funds or certificates of deposit. (You don't want to be caught by a bear market or a recession just before high school.) By the time your teen starts their senior year of high school, you'll have at least the first year of post-high school expenses in a CD.

Speaking as a rookie grandparent, I'm looking forward to watching Carol build her kid's 529 account.

I'm also looking forward to Carol teaching her daughter another skill that was a big deal in our family: working on a big project for just 20 minutes a day.

CAROL
"All Hail 20 Minutes A Day"

Mom has a lot of stories from her days as a young woman at a military academy. One of the memorable ones was about preparing for a test in a freshman class. In the weeks (not days) leading up to the test, she spent just 20 minutes a day studying. The night before the test when she planned her final study session, she got a huge surprise: an upperclassman placed her "on duty" manning a watch station for the next few hours, simply because her roommate hadn't shown up for their assigned watch. The three hours Mom had scheduled that evening to study were gone, just like that. As furious as anyone would be about losing precious study time the night before the test, Mom was also really glad she'd spent the last few weeks studying for the test a little at a time. Despite the loss of time, she aced the test.

"All hail 20 minutes a day" became a mantra in the Nordman household around the time I started elementary school, because that's when I started getting "real" homework and projects. Twenty minutes was about the same time as a TV show, and I could do anything for just one TV show. But like any normal kid, I didn't follow the mantra. There were a handful of late nights where I'd neglected a project until the last minute, or when I decided to just do a marathon "cramming session" with classmates instead of a little studying every day.

In my teen years I was very bad at tackling my finances in 20 minute-a-day increments (you'll hear more about "Money Day" later). But I've since learned in my ultra-busy adult life that 20 minutes a day really makes money more manageable, especially when my personal life only fits into the "spare time" after my military job.

On the flip side, Mom and Dad continued to execute 20 minutes a day in all kinds of teachable moments. Dad spent just 20 minutes one day creating the famed Kid 401(k) spreadsheet, which was always ready to open whenever I asked about it. Dad tracked all of the family finances in Quicken, the equivalent of a digital check register before "auto-sync" was invented, by spending just 20 minutes entering the day's spending. In the 20 minutes it took for me to ride the bus home from school, Mom and Dad would sit down in their living room recliners and enjoy the last 20 minutes of peace together before their daughter "Hurricane Carol" rolled through the door. It always made me super happy to come home from a long day at school and see my parents happily chatting away, ready to welcome me home and hear about my day.

To help achieve your 20 minutes a day, use your smartphone apps and your to-do list to your advantage. Can you take 5 minutes to clean out your wallet of all the receipts and put them in a monthly envelope on your desk or table? Can you take another 5 minutes to set your credit cards on auto-pay? How about another 5 minutes to set an auto-transfer from your checking account to your savings? And maybe the last 5 minutes writing the grocery list as you comb through the fridge and kitchen cabinets for dinner ingredients?

Boom, those four tasks add up to 20 minutes. All Hail 20 Minutes A Day.

What are the 20 minutes-a-day tasks that your kids can master now to establish positive habits in spending, saving, and time management?

SUMMARY
The Earlier You Start, The Easier (And Cheaper) It Gets.

Carol and I both know now that starting a family can seem like a gigantic, costly, intimidating project. Once you've made the decision and held that baby in your arms, you'll figure out the rest one day at a time.

The techniques that get you to financial independence will also help you cut the expense of raising your family, and along the way you'll teach them money-savvy skills for their future. Give them a safe and loving environment for them to make their money mistakes, and for you to help them figure out how to manage it better.

Don't get distracted by analysis paralysis and don't overthink it. There's never a perfect time to do it, but you can always find 20 minutes a day. Start the education fund early and begin letting your kids experiment with money.

CHAPTER GOALS

- Let your kids make money mistakes.
- Establish your kids' education fund and start saving now.
- Teach kids about money in just 20 minutes a day.

CHAPTER TWO

Your Child Is Ready To Learn To Manage Their Money When They Stop Eating It

> **"**
>
> WE KNEW WHEN IT WAS
> TIME TO START TEACHING
> YOU ABOUT MONEY.
>
> MARGE AND DOUG NORDMAN

**FINANCIAL TERMS AND CONCEPTS
IN THIS CHAPTER**

- Handling money (safely).
- Being allowed to buy "One Special Thing" during shopping trips.

DOUG
Learning About Money
By Talking About It

When our daughter was 18 months old, she learned about money by eating a quarter.

No excuses: it was one of my careless parenting moments. I left a quarter near her, and she picked it up. As toddlers do, she put it into her mouth for a taste.

She began choking on it.

You know those parenting posters where they show you holding a choking child upside-down and gently thumping their back to clear their airway? That happens very fast when you're quietly freaking out and suddenly full of adrenaline. My "gentle" thump helped our little darling cough that coin over six feet.

When she was putting money in her mouth, she wasn't ready to learn how to manage it yet. Apparently I wasn't ready to manage money around a toddler, either.

But a few months later when she stopped eating money and started talking in sentences, then we started talking about money. We're still talking about it.

My spouse and I will admit up front (and for the rest of our lives!) that we were occasionally terrified parents. By our daughter's second birthday we knew that we had a fireball on our hands. We had to think and plan ahead of her to help guide her boundless energy before she ran amok. She was endlessly curious in the up-front, in-your-face way of many toddlers, and we knew that we needed answers. A lot of answers.

We knew that we were supposed to talk with her. The best way was to talk about whatever we parents were doing at the moment, and we told her that she'd be able to do those things, too — when she was old enough.

When we talked about using money, we started with buying "one special thing." It was our daughter's choice what that thing would be, but no matter what, it would only be one thing.

We survived many trips to the grocery store with this reminder: "If you behave then you can buy One Special Thing when we finish shopping. But if you don't behave then you can't buy anything and we're going home."

"One Special Thing" helped our toddler learn deferred gratification. (Even for a piece of candy.) She (mostly) behaved at the store by remembering that there was a reward at the end.

She occasionally tested the system. We dealt with a couple of epic meltdowns. Once we even had to rapidly retreat to the store's parking lot to calm down and regain control.

One Special Thing is also a teachable moment about choices. Maybe your child is only allowed to buy an item which costs less than a dollar, or maybe it has to be a healthy snack. Maybe it's not even food but rather a book or a small toy. While Marge and I talked about what Carol was going to buy we added in experiences like holding two dollars, or we said that our family had enough money to buy food and clothes and One Special Thing. We even mentioned that for a really big One Special Thing she'd need to save a lot of money or have a really good job.

The same tactic worked at garage sales and thrift stores. We gave our youngster a few dollars and let her figure out what she could buy with her money. She made impulsive decisions, not rational ones. She gradually learned to control her emotions and manage her money.

We had entire discussions about where we got the money, how much things cost, and what would bring value to her life. "Do you want this book that you can read over and over at bedtime, or do you want this small toy? Do you think you'll play with it a lot and it'll last forever, or will you get tired of it? Do you want to wear this t-shirt instead?"

Her actual choices were less important than using the 5Ws and How to make her choices. The whole purpose of our conversations was to help her think about her money and what she could do with it, and then to guide her through her thoughts and feelings.

Remember the analogy of your kids running around the yard lighting $20 bills on fire like Fourth of July sparklers. They're still going to do that when they're older, but you can start working on their financial thoughts now. Later, it'll also help manage the meltdowns when they run out of money.

Over 25 years later, we're still joking about One Special Thing when our daughter faces major decisions like buying a vehicle.

In her next section, Carol will share more ways that our family talked about money.

CAROL
All the Lights And Sounds

I found myself slowly and quietly picking my jaw off the floor as I read the above story. I, um, didn't know that I once choked on a quarter as a kid. Thanks for rescuing me from my first of MANY poor money decisions, Dad!

Let's backpedal for a moment to the part where Dad said "...when she started talking in sentences, then we started talking about money." My parents did not literally start talking to an 18-month-old about what a penny is. What really happened not long after the quarter incident was that:

Mom and Dad started creating positive, understandable experiences with money, so that I would have positive, understandable ideas about money.

And that's the key concept: give your child a positive, understandable experience with money. Like Marie Kondo says when it comes to organizing your life, working with your money should "spark joy," and that joy is something only developed through positive, understandable experiences and happy thoughts.

The aim is to appreciate the money's potential, not material possessions. With the One Special Thing, a kid learns what money can buy (a new toy or candy), and what money cannot buy (... everything!). When a child handles bills or coins or a plastic card—

even if it's just for a moment's entertainment—they should find money fun to play with. Money shouldn't be something that gets kids in trouble when they touch it. Money should be something that they feel comfortable around; something that they feel confident or even powerful with.

Like all parenting techniques, letting a kid play with money is:

1) Done in baby steps,

2) Adjusted to the pace of the individual child, and

3) Repeated as necessary until the child truly "gets it," whatever "it" means in this particular lesson.

So here's what you do instead of buying everything for your kids.

To begin, under your direct supervision, let your child simply play with a coin or two. Let them gaze at the shiny silver and copper color, finger the little pictures and faces on the sides of the coins, even try to squish the coin in their palm tight enough so that the little faces and figures dent their skin. Let them color on the coins with crayons or paint, and trace the coins on paper. An older sibling or cousin could show them how to roll the coins across a smooth surface, or spin the coins, or play tiddly-winks. Answer all of the creative and weird questions they may ask about the coins. Just let them have fun and create a positive memory with physical money.

When I proved to my parents that I wouldn't eat coins (anymore), they gave me a small present: a playset of plastic coins shaped like American money. The coins came in a small plastic cash register. There was only one (other) rule with the toy money: when I was done playing with them, I had to "clean up my coins" by putting them back in the little cash register drawer when I was done.

Little did I know that this was the very first step of "keeping track of your money," and we'll come back to this concept again...and again... and again...

When I decided to play with my coins, my parents would closely supervise me. They would watch what I did with them, answer any weird questions I asked, and maybe throw a suggestion or two my way. Why don't I try sorting the coins by color? How about by size? Why not put the piles in order from smallest coins to largest coin? Why not make little stacks out of my piles? As they say in the old AT&T commercials, my parents were slowly "raising the bar." And I learned that I actually liked the little games of organizing and comparing coins.

The next thing my parents did was very sneaky. With 20/20 hindsight, it was downright ninja parenting. When my parents saw I had finished sorting piles, they would ask me how many coins I had in each pile. When I looked up at them with confused eyes, they would sit down next to me and teach me how to count. They would touch each coin with a finger, and say three little words: One...two...three! One...two...three! Over and over and over again.

And when I could count to three without a mistake, my parents taught me to count to five. When I could count to five, my parents taught me how to count to ten, and so on. Soon I could count all of my coins. It's a little funny how fake coins magically turned into an incredibly cheap educational tool. And I thought I was still playing around!

Over several years, I slowly learned more and more about my coins. When my parents saw that I recognized the different coin sizes, they started to teach me what each coin meant. The brown ones are pennies. Each penny is one. I can count my pennies: one, two, three...

The baby-baby grey ones are dimes. Each dime is ten. Ten, twenty, thirty...

With almost no effort, I could now count, talk about colors, and recognize coins. And I was only four years old.

Whoa.

Dollar bills are a different story. Dollar bills are too easy to crumple, too flimsy to withstand the destructive nature of the average "three-nager." As a former three-nager, I just wasn't ready to handle such fancy paper. But my parents took every opportunity to *show me what to do with dollars*. When the family ate out at McDonald's, they would take me with them to the cash register, lifted me up to the counter so that I could see, and would say, "Look! See all that yummy food? See how I give the nice lady my dollar, and she gives me these yummy chicken nuggets? It's really cool, huh?! Would you like some chicken nuggets, too?" I learned that if I gave the nice lady this special green money—this whole "doll-ar"—I would get some tasty food in return. Another positive memory and lesson about money was formed.

In this modern, cashless society, it's almost unnatural to whip out bills, assuming you're actually carrying cash in the first place. So how do you demonstrate cash transactions to kids?

Start by making little transactions with cash. Fancy a trip to the corner ice cream shop? Bring along some cash and have the kids hand the money over at the register. Going out to get groceries? Pay for the bulk of the groceries as you usually do, whether a credit card, a smart phone app, or check, and point out to the kids "how big" the total price is. Kids will slowly learn that the "big" price is "too big" for the cash on hand. If they can handle the math, have them notice that $23.40 is more than the $20.00 in cash they're holding. If your kid is visual, type it up on your phone or write it down on a scrap of receipt if it helps.

But, after paying the "big" bulk price transaction, set aside one or two small things where you—and maybe even your kid—will use cash. That way, kids can see the different ways to use money, and maybe even form another positive money and social experience by interacting with the cashier or self-service machine.

If your kid turns out to be wildly independent and somewhat capable (but not perfect), then let them choose the small transaction item: the One Special Thing. Point out the price to them on the shelf, and verbalize it. For example, say "look there! This pack of candy is 85 cents. With taxes, that's almost a dollar. We'll pay for it with cash at the register." And then follow through by letting your kid pay for it with cash at the register.

SUMMARY
Just Keep Talking With Your Child

It might be hard to find the mental energy when you're barely functioning in between meals and diaper changes. You're certainly not going to hold up your end of a dissertation on developmental milestones.

What you can do is engage your toddler's attention. Keep talking with them and show them how to communicate. When they start using toddler words then you'll help them form sentences. You'll talk about everything that you see and do together, and eventually you'll start talking about paying for things with money. They'll learn at their own pace, as long as you keep talking with them.

In the next chapter we'll talk about the preschool years.

CHAPTER GOALS

- Keep talking with your kids about everything you see and do together.
- Teach kids to handle and store money and count it.
- Use "One Special Thing" to help kids learn to make choices about using money.

CHAPTER THREE

Managing Allowances, Chores, and Jobs

> ❝
>
> (With a Jamaican Accent)
> GET A JOB, MON!
>
> **KEENEN IVORY WAYANS**
> *IN LIVING COLOR*, THE TV SHOW

- Allowances—being a good member of the family.
- Chores—age-appropriate tasks as a good member of the family, no compensation.
- Jobs—age-appropriate tasks to earn money, once chores are done.
- Kids learn how to manage money by making mistakes.

DOUG
Allowances, Chores, And Jobs

Remember our analogy in Chapter 1 about kids running around with flaming $20 bills? The learning starts here.

Allowances are a controversial topic. Each family holds different opinions about whether or not a kid "deserves" an allowance. However, an allowance can also be a guaranteed learning experience. You parents will set your own policies for how much to save, how much to give, and how much to spend—or even whether you want to hand out allowances at all!

We're not suggesting what standards to choose, yet an allowance is one of the best ways for your kids to get their hands on money. They'll make spending choices and learn about the consequences.

Our ulterior parenting motive was giving our daughter regular chances to learn how to handle ever-larger sums of money. An allowance was just one tool for that, along with other responsibilities and opportunities around the house.

We told our daughter a simple story: you get an allowance for being a good member of the family. We never really defined "good member of the family" and there were no strings attached. We started with a weekly allowance and (years later) stretched that out to monthly.

How much of an allowance will you give your kids? Ask yourselves: how much wasteful spending can you tolerate while letting them make their own mistakes?

You want it to be big enough to give them the opportunity to spend their own money every week, yet small enough to force them to make choices.

When our daughter was a preschooler (and stopped eating money), we started with three quarters per week. We raised it a little at every birthday until she was a teen, and after that we began giving her more control over her part of the family budget.

Another important part of starting an allowance is building trust. Your kid has to know that it comes regularly. They have to know that their money is someplace safe (a piggy bank, wallet, or purse) and that they can access it whenever they want. As they grow older you'll introduce the concepts of bank accounts and certificates of deposit, but they have to believe that your family bank can also be trusted. You have to keep their deposits safe (or keep good records) and you have to honor the bank's rules for withdrawals.

As parents, my wife and I also decided that our daughter's allowance did not depend on chores or behavior... or really anything at all. We wanted her to learn to handle money and how to manage it. We wanted her to have just enough reliable income to be forced to make financial choices.

Everybody in the family has to do chores every day to keep the household neat and clean and a nice place to live. We told Carol that chores taught her to take care of her things and that they'd help her become a smart grownup in charge of her own house. We started her with anything that was simple and short and fun to do with us—especially putting away toys and clothes, unloading groceries, or fetching the mail.

We found other ways to motivate our daughter to do her age-appropriate parts of our household chores. We used lots of shelves and boxes to make it easy for her to see her toys and her clothing and to clean up. We used the chores chart for reminders and to let her check them off as she did them. If she wanted to have fun (like going to the park) then she had to finish her chores. If she neglected her chores, TV and electronics privileges might be suspended.

The next incentive for chores was that if she wanted to earn more money by doing **jobs**, then she had to finish her **chores** first. **Jobs** were her choice, but **chores** were mandatory.

Jobs are an exercise in financial motivation. The goal behind jobs around the house is encouraging success at earning money. Like the old skit from the TV show "In Living Color," when Carol wanted a new toy or popular clothing we used to joke "Get a job, mon!" She quickly learned to stop begging and to start thinking about how to earn the money to buy it herself.

Jobs have to be useful (like washing the wheels on the car or sweeping the sidewalk) but not the child's routine chores. (Jobs are only for when the kid chooses to earn money.) It also has to be age-appropriate, and it might start with just 15 minutes of focus for a dollar or two. Even if a preschooler is cleaning a small part of the car with Mom or Dad, a kid should enjoy their feelings of accomplishment as much as they enjoy the cash in their hands. Some training and supervision has to go into doing the job right, and lots of praise has to follow.

Of course, it's perfectly fine for parents to offer to occasionally outsource their Mom and Dad chores as kid jobs. (Parents just have to be willing to budget their money to pay for it!) However, the kids have to keep their privilege of accepting the opportunity. If they don't want the money then they don't have to do the job.

Jobs are a great way to teach kids about trading their life energy for money, and aligning their spending to the things which they really value. Kids will quickly learn to make smart choices about their opportunities. They'll also figure out how hard they're willing to work for that toy or experience.

How did we know when our daughter was ready to tackle allowances, chores, and jobs?

Well...we didn't always know that she was ready, but we used trial and error. Sometimes there was more error than trial.

During the preschool years she just wanted to be a big kid like the ones she saw in every book and video and around the neighborhood. When we tried out an allowance and chores, we talked about how our family did this to help her learn to be a big kid. We kept talking about money every time she showed interest or did something with her allowance. We helped with a chore when she needed it, and we backed off to supervise when she wanted to do it herself.

Her jobs grew out of watching us parents do our chores. If she was interested in a job (or motivated to earn money for a toy) then we worked alongside her and paid her an amount appropriate with her help. Washing a car was a lot of fun, even if she could only handle cleaning the wheels. Painting a wall? She was all over that job, or at least what she could reach from the ground. The first jobs were usually messy and quality came later, but she was always learning to be a big kid.

If she couldn't handle something then we'd talk about it, and maybe we'd try it again. If it was a miserable failure then we'd quietly move on to something else. We'd wait a few months until everyone was older (and smarter) and then we'd try a different way to develop the skill.

As our daughter grew older and started talking about all the things she wanted to buy, we'd remind her of the old Keenen Ivory Wayans skit: "Get a *job*, mon!"

I should clarify that our system of allowances, chores, and jobs was not always smooth sailing.

There was still plenty of negotiation and rebellion in our house. We tried to keep the rules simple and clear. If Carol wanted to have fun she had to follow the rules.

No matter how many times she challenged authority, she was still learning how to take care of her money and make spending choices. We parents had to remember that.

CAROL
Jobs For...What, Exactly?

Kids will find plenty of opportunities to spend money. I remember the neighborhood ice cream truck (year round in our tropical neighborhood), the Scholastic Book Fairs at school, and all the games that were coming out for the new Gameboy Color. That didn't include a new basketball, a new soccer ball, a Razor scooter, and so on. There were plenty of "gimmies" (from the phrase "give me") for me to want and thus plenty of ways for me to run out of money. So as I got older and my gimmies grew, I wanted more job opportunities.

By the time I could read, Mom started keeping a running list of jobs to do around the house. That way, if I suddenly wanted to do a job—like after a TV commercial advertising the latest Pokemon cards—Mom and I could sit down with the list and choose one or a few jobs to work on and earn money. The list was always handy on the counter, so I could open the discussion with Mom and Dad almost any time the desire struck.

DOUG
Teachable Moments

The easiest teachable moment was making change. When she got her weekly allowance then we showed her the choices: dollar bills, quarters, dimes, nickels, or even... pennies?

At first, preschoolers think that two hundred pennies are worth more than a couple of boring paper dollar bills. Quantity is value!

We tried to include our daughter in as many financial discussions as she could handle. When we were at the grocery store (with the One Special Thing rule lurking in the background) we talked about choices. We talked about having jobs and earning enough money to pay for things. We talked about whether we made good choices and what would happen if you made "other" choices.

We also tried to let her handle the money tools. We'd let her put the ATM card into the machine, and show her how its computer could "read" the card like she could read a book. We talked about how the bank stored our money (in the ATM, of course!) and would give it back to us when we asked for it. If the stores weren't too busy then we'd show her how to run our credit card through the cashier's terminal and how to watch the numbers.

CAROL
Coins Are Easy To Lose

Another lesson I'd forgotten I learned is that coins are easy to lose. They get stuck in the bottom of pockets, they slip out of your wallet when you accidentally turn it upside down, and sometimes they just plain disappear, no matter how close a watch you keep over your change.

One of the methods that really worked for me as a kid was to have a coin bank that sorted my coins by type, rather than creating a heaping, mixed pile of change. One of the early money books I received was *The Money Book and Hideaway Bank: A Smart Kid's Guide to Savvy Saving and Spending* by Wyatt and Hinden. I've long outgrown *The Money Book*, but the Hideaway Bank still holds my spare change to this day. It's a plastic bank in the shape of a one-inch book with a clear window on one side, and with dividers to keep different kinds of coins and bills separated. The top of the bank has a sliding door, making the change accessible when I'm ready to withdraw it.

Another method is to have a bank divided by category of money, instead of type of change. Kids can have goals for different categories, like "saving," "One Special Thing," or even specific goals like "new baseball jersey." Kids will get a kick out of seeing all the change pile up, and can tangibly tie their stored change to a future goal.

SUMMARY
Figure Out Your Plan And Watch For Those Teachable Moments.

All those years ago when we parents started talking about allowances, chores, and jobs, we had no idea that the vocabulary would continue until our child was a young adult. Even today, Carol and I say to each other "Wow, you'll have to get a really good job to afford that!"

However you decide to put money in the hands of your kids, give them every opportunity to practice managing their assets. Help them discuss their feelings, and work through "what if?" scenarios. At this age it's all about getting their hands on things and seeing an immediate result for their actions. It's also a great chance to let them make small mistakes and then talk about their feelings.

Once you've figured out the rules then you can give them the tools: coins, banks, and toys (like the Hideaway Bank) to help them learn money management through playing with it. We'll share more tools in later chapters.

CHAPTER GOALS

- Decide if, when, and how much you'll give as allowances.
- Assign age-appropriate chores for your kids.
- Offer job opportunities (after chores are done!) to help kids learn to be entrepreneurs and manage money.
- Practice finding teachable moments about managing money.

CHAPTER FOUR

Starting Grade School—And Shopping!

> **"**
>
> GONDOR PRIMULON.
>
> *RECESS*, THE TV SHOW

**FINANCIAL TERMS AND CONCEPTS
IN THIS CHAPTER**

- Learning how to buy with thrift stores, garage sales, and fast-food restaurants.
- Dealing with Disney: shopping versus buying.
- Certificates of Deposit (CDs) in your family bank at one penny per dollar per month.

DOUG
Starting School

Every parent looks forward to the day that their kid starts elementary school! It's the first time that they're really building their reading and math skills and learning what grownups do all day.

As parents, this is your chance to leverage their learning with even more financial literacy. Your kids can learn how to do more with money whether you're homeschooling, going to the local public school, or attending a private school. They might be ready by kindergarten, or they might wait until third grade before showing interest, but school is full of opportunities.

This is also the time when "peer tutoring" really kicks in. Kids show up on the first day with different skills and readiness. Some are already reading and writing while others will catch up with the rest of the class. They're all learning from each other, and the peer pressure starts: not just in reading and school games but also in fashion, toys, and tech.

Their socializing expands and they pick up new behaviors. They might decide to have their recess indoors making up weird slogans. (Like the nerdy kids in the Recess TV show that made this chapter's epigraph.) Or they'll go outside to enjoy the day with the cool kids. This is their time to form their own social networks and decide who they want as friends.

Peer pressure has a poor reputation from all the bad choices that kids can make. However it's also one more parental tool for encouraging better behavior. ("See how the other kids are playing well with each other? Would you like to have fun with them, too? Remember your manners and try to share!") It's a powerful tool for developing social skills.

Your child also develops new material interests from their friends. Everyone falls prey to consumer advertising and clever marketing tactics, but eventually most of us learn that the commercials look better than the actual toy.

It's a whole new world full of choices, and parents can help kids think their way through the best options.

By the time Carol started school, she'd received an allowance for a couple of years and she knew the rules. She kept her money in a small bank in her room, or in a wallet. Once in a while she'd give it to us to keep safe for her, and we built on her trust by promptly returning it when she asked for it.

She usually kept up with her chores and would occasionally be interested in earning more money for a toy or a game. Our reminder of "chores before jobs" was enough to keep her motivated. We got a lot of help with yardwork, washing cars, and painting around the house. It could get messy and we had to focus on training as well as quality, but she was usually good for 30-45 minutes of focused effort.

She was also learning a lot about fast food, shopping, buying Disney souvenirs, and paying for her purchases.

When Carol started elementary school she was tall enough to see over the counter at McDonald's. Marge and I had to be patient with this teachable moment, but we'd usually get a chance near the end of the meal. After everyone had eaten their food and had quality time in the play area, we'd ask her if she wanted some ice cream. Once we had her full attention then we'd talk through how to order a cone, how to give the money to the cashier, and how much change she should get back. At first we'd go with her to the counter, but within a few trips she'd learned how to take the money and do the transaction on her own.

CAROL
A Little Money For A Big Treat and A Big Lesson

While growing up, I loved ice cream, especially the plain vanilla soft serve at McDonald's. Once I was tall enough to see over the counter, and could hold small objects without dropping them (like dollars and coins), Mom and Dad taught me how to order my own ice cream. One parent—usually Mom—would take me to a table near the register (and away from the distractions of the family table and the McDonald's playground), teach me to say, "May I have an ice cream cone, please?" and give me the exact change. Mom would watch me from the table as I scampered right up to the register, held out my handful of coins to the cashier, and said in my big little kid voice, "May I have a cone, please?" If the cashier didn't understand me, they would glance at Mom. Mom would then say to me, but in a loud voice that the cashier could hear, "Carol, I think you mean you want an ice cream cone, please." The cashier got the drift and started pressing buttons while I "shouted out" my sentence once more. About a minute later, I happily returned to Mom, licking my ice cream cone.

Between ages 4 and 8, the routine of buying an ice cream cone changed as my financial literacy improved. By the time I was in first grade, I could be trusted to go to the register alone, without Mom waiting nearby. By the time I was in second grade, I could add and subtract with speed; instead of giving me exact change, Mom and Dad gave me whole bills. I would count the change at the register, and then bring back the change and the receipt to Mom and Dad. Then, Mom and Dad would ask me to count the change again and check it against the receipt. By the time I was in the third grade, Mom and Dad trusted me to count change without their verification. Also by the time I was 8, my allowance was big enough that I could pay for my own ice cream, and maybe even upgrade to a McFlurry™—a bigger cup of soft serve ice cream with candy or cookie chunks mixed into it.

By the time I was 10, Mom and Dad didn't even bother ordering when we visited McDonald's. They'd walk in, sit down at a table they liked, tell me their orders, hand me a couple of $20 bills, and watch me approach the register by myself. It was a (patient) test to see if I could handle money, listen, and remember orders. It wasn't until years later that I realized they were growing my ability to *ahem* provide food for myself and—if I chose to have my own spouse and kids one day—provide food for them, too. At the very least, I was capable of feeding myself if my parents weren't around.

So, if I could count my money, and I could buy my own food, what else could my parents pawn off—I mean "delegate"—to me to do? The possibilities were growing.

DOUG
Shopping

School also meant more shopping for clothes: more garage sales and thrift stores!

Carol had been shopping in these places all of her life, but now some of Carol's school friends didn't want to wear "old dirty clothes" from other people. ("Eeew, you don't know where those clothes really came from!?!") We talked about how you could spend $15 for one t-shirt at the mall or you could buy 4 or 5 of them at a thrift store—and some of them were nearly new! She could get the same Disney characters or fancy designs that she saw at school or on TV without paying the prices of a "real Disney store."

When we shopped at major department stores (as people had to do back in the 1990s before Amazon emerged) we'd point out how much clothing and toys cost. We'd talk about the amount of money that we had in the budget for them, and then figure out our choices. We'd compare them to the bargains she could find at thrift stores and garage sales and explain that the bargains gave us more money in our budget to save and invest. On the other hand, if she wanted to shop at the mall for her clothes then she'd need to have a really good job and save her money.

By now, at ages 6 through 8, she was old enough to have a conversation with other adults and to focus on a transaction without (too much) parental supervision. When we got to the checkout counter she could usually talk with the cashier and help with swiping a credit card or paying cash. If she was spending her own allowance or job money for a toy then she could do it with us. She was also old enough to tell when the other grownups were impressed (or surprised) that she was handling the purchase.

Here's another suggestion for teaching kids to manage money: mobile deposit. It wasn't around for us parents during the last millennium, but today a kid is perfectly capable of learning how to use a smartphone to deposit a paper check for Mom or Dad.

> TODAY A KID IS PERFECTLY CAPABLE OF LEARNING HOW TO USE A SMART-PHONE TO DEPOSIT A PAPER CHECK FOR MOM OR DAD.

Whether young adults are using paper checks today is a different discussion, but we still get a few checks in the mail. This is an opportunity to show them how the money moves around. If you need to deposit a check, you can hand your (logged in) phone over to your child and supervise them as they endorse the check (the parent signs, of course) and submit the deposit. When the deposit is complete, show them how the numbers in your checking account changed with that transaction.

CAROL
SHOPPING!!!

Now let's go back to garage sales. Garage sales are a surprisingly good opportunity to teach kids a ton of life skills without the high risk of taking kids to a "real" store. To list a few reasons why garage sales offer teachable moments:

- Garage sales are usually on weekend mornings, when kids are already up and running about and looking for something to do.

- Garage sales are kid-friendly setups. Most sales happen on the ground or on lower tables, so kids can browse more easily than in a department store where shelves are frequently double or triple their height and the urge to climb is just too strong for anyone's safety.

- Kids are easier to supervise at garage sales. Thanks to the lack of hiding spots, it's easier to keep an eye on the kids while they're roaming around the items for sale.

- Kids are easier to peel away from garage sales. If any temper tantrums erupt or accidents happen or there's just too many people around, it's a lot easier to just drop whatever you're holding (literally) and address the issue, or even remove the kid from the scene until they're in control of themselves again.

- Kids learn how to "look but not touch" or how to "ask nicely before trying something on." And in more extreme cases, kids learn the "you break it, you pay for it" rule for a far cheaper cost at a garage sale than at many stores.

- Garage sales are quieter. There's no rattle of carts, no announcements or advertisements blaring over loudspeakers overhead, no cash registers ringing and dinging. Some garage sales may attract attention with booming music, but shoppers can easily walk up to the host and ask for a lower volume.

- Kids can meet your neighbors. The local garage sale attracts a lot of neighbors, so both you and your kid can meet the neighborhood and/or practice how to deal with strangers. I made a couple of new playmates in the neighborhood via garage sales.

- Heaven forbid a kid should steal right under your nose, but if they do, there's a real person—not a faceless corporation or a stern police officer— they have to face when returning the stolen item with an apology.

- Kids can gain confidence in making good choices by shopping at A LOT of garage sales—again, bad but necessary choices are cheaper at garage sales than at stores!

The only major disadvantage of garage sales is that they're infrequent nowadays. Thanks to Craigslist, Facebook Marketplace and Buy/Sell/Trade Groups, Amazon.com, and the steady increase in thrift shop donations, garage sales don't occur as much anymore.

One alternative is the local market, whether a Farmer's Market, Swap Meet, or Flea Market. Some neighborhoods will host a community yard sale—usually in a local parking lot or field—where people can sell their items in a common location. These options largely depend on their quality, availability, and your opinion of their safety, especially if they are in high traffic, maze-like, or run-down areas you're not comfortable bringing your progeny to.

Another option is to visit your local thrift store. Like garage sales, thrift stores are a great way to teach kids basic life skills with low risk. Sure, thrift stores are noisier than garage sales, and many thrift stores are HUGE and filled with many good hiding spots and climbable shelves. But again, the "you break it, you pay for it" rule is far easier to learn in a thrift shop, and a bustling thrift shop environment is still much less hectic than the packed Target or Walmart. Some Thrift Shops have gone so far as to create a "try-it" section for kids' toys, also serving as a great distraction to keep kids calm while parents shop.

Nowadays, I earn my own (pretty good) paycheck, but I still choose to shop at Target, Ross Dress for Less (my favorite!), thrift stores, and Amazon.com for clothes. Now that I'm no longer a kid constantly growing and changing sizes, I find value in buying a $30 dress off the rack at Ross that lasts for decades. I've also learned that I'm more successful in finding clothes I like in my size at Ross than I am in finding the $5 version at the thrift shop or the $150 version at the local department store. But like all money lessons, this was a lesson learned over two-ish decades of buying my own clothes (combining WHAT and WHEN and HOW), and accelerated by shopping on my own in middle school, high school, and college. For reasons I don't understand, I've only found good business suits at Ross and thrift shops.

Pinterest is another unexpectedly wonderful shopping tool. As a kid growing up, I was never quite sure what my style was, and the worst place to learn what my style is was in a busy store where everything around me pressured me to "buy it all....buy it all...buy it all...." So instead of stepping into a brick-and-mortar location, I look to Pinterest to find inspiration and to *ahem* pin down exactly what kind of style I like. I also love how I can pin something I like on Pinterest, no matter how cheap or expensive the look is, and come back to that idea year after year as styles change and the fashion industry updates. This can serve as a lesson for your children in planning and deciding what they really want when it is time to go shopping for school clothes.

Pinterest works for toys and other "gimme" urges for all ages. I have a board on Pinterest called "gimmies." Every time I see something that I WANT, but really don't NEED, I take a picture and/or scan in the barcode, and save it to my Pinterest board. Most of the time, I find I've lost interest in the item when I've left the store. Other times, I find that my gimmie board makes the perfect list for my friends and husband to use when trying to buy holiday gifts for me.

DOUG
Dealing With Disney

When our family went on our first Disney trip, we parents knew that we'd experience aggressive marketing. Marge and I thought we were ready, but even as grownups we were overwhelmed by the choices.

We were in trouble at the very first souvenir shop on Main Street.

(Luckily the staff left us alone.) Carol saw all the cool gear and had a huge case of the gimmies: she wanted to spend every penny of her savings on everything she saw in the first few minutes. When we started to talk about prices and choices, there were tears and a minor meltdown. (It wasn't just me— Carol was unhappy too!) Amid all of that emotional stress, Marge gets the credit for a brilliantly creative tactic.

Once everyone calmed down, she told Carol about the difference between "shopping" and "buying." Instead of arguing about what to buy, we decided that we'd spend the first two days only on shopping: looking at all the choices and adding her favorites to a list. On the third day, she'd look at everything on her list one more time and make her buying choices.

It eliminated all of her souvenir stress. She happily spent a few minutes checking out each store, but she also enjoyed the rides and the shows. We parents heaved a huge sigh of relief, knowing that she wouldn't be crazed by all of the choices.

CAROL
The Disney T-Shirt Trick

Mom and Dad weren't kidding about "making it up as they go along." Sometimes they realized that they had a teachable moment unfolding right at that moment. But as I got older, and formed a more distinctive personality, Mom and Dad became good enough to predict teachable moments months in advance. A great example of this is the Disney t-shirt trick.

On the night before we went into Disneyland, we were settling into the local hotel and planning out the next day's adventure. Mom and Dad surprised me with a small present: several Disney t-shirts in my size and tastes, enough to wear a "new" Disney shirt every day at the park. I was ecstatic, thankful for the gifts, and even more excited to run around Disneyland in my new t-shirts. I was far more eager to spend the day on rides and walking through the park instead of "finding souvenirs" and risking another meltdown.

It wasn't until years later that Mom spilled the beans about where those t-shirts actually came from. In the months before Disneyland, Mom made multiple trips to the local Goodwill until she found enough t-shirts for me for the whole vacation. I had no idea that had happened, and better yet, I didn't care where the t-shirts had come from! After all those years, it meant more to me that I had "that experience" of proudly showing off my t-shirts than it did to say where the t-shirts came from.

So what if your kid wasn't as easily distracted as I was, and still wanted to go shopping? Mom and Dad were willing to let me into any and every Disney store, BUT I had to keep a list of the things I wanted and at which store I would find them. Nowadays I would run around snapping photos with a smartphone camera. At the end of the week, I would choose one thing from my list, and Mom and Dad would take me to that store to buy it. While Mom and Dad were willing to buy One Special Thing, I had to pay for any additional things I wanted. I quickly figured out that I couldn't afford much in the Disney stores.

 DOUG

Gifts From Relatives And Saving at the Bank Of Carol

Gifts from relatives should be easier to handle after dealing with fast food, shopping, and Disney. This is a teachable moment when kids can learn how to save and invest for their purchases, and then make sure they have enough money to pay for them.

During elementary school, relatives considered Carol old enough to start getting "serious money" for birthdays and holidays. $20 made a big difference to her discretionary spending, and we tried to use all the opportunities we encountered.

We talked about her choices in spending, saving, or giving. It was easy to remind her of the shopping and buying that we did at Disneyland. With her new school skills, she could write down her ideas and her choices and make her own lists.

"Saving" was a stretch for a youngster who was still learning impulse control. As David Owen points out in *First National Bank Of Dad*, kids want to control their money. If parents confiscate a kid's birthday money for "savings" (or, even worse, "the college fund") then from the kid's perspective their parents are crazy. In that situation, the kid's only rational control over their money is spending it before it gets taken away from them.

But what if a kid could use that money to make more money? Maybe it's unreasonable to expect a kid to practice delayed gratification for a far-off goal like college. (Let alone retirement!) On the other hand, it might be reasonable to pay a kid to save and invest their money. Once again, we parents would have to help Carol build trust in our family banking system.

When we talked about all the things she could do with her new birthday wealth, we suggested using some of it to start a "certificate of deposit" at a bank. We kept it simple, though, by calling it a CD at the Bank of Carol.

Young kids take a while to learn about percentages, so this bank's CD paid a penny per dollar per month. One perCENT per month or 12% per year.

Every grownup wants to earn 12% annual interest on their investments, especially when they can redeem the CD at any time with no penalties!

We even updated her CD balance in Quicken, the same software we used to track our family finances. Every month I entered the interest, and we'd show her the computer screen or print out a summary. Today we'd probably track these numbers on a family-friendly system of debit cards with tablets or smartphones, but kids can still keep a paper statement. They can enjoy holding a physical piece of paper in their hands, or taping it up in their bedroom as a hardcopy reminder.

We told our daughter that this was a great return on her money, but once again we had to build credibility and trust. During the rest of the year she tested the system occasionally by asking to withdraw all of her deposits. We promptly complied—in cash—with dollar bills and the correct change (down to the penny). Once she was holding her net worth in her hands, we'd point out how much interest she could earn next month and ask her what she wanted to do with all of that money. Our discussions usually ended with her returning her funds for more interest, but the whole experience let her build trust and confidence in her bank.

Of course she still had to do math and make sure she had enough to afford her purchases.

CAROL
Trusting the Bank of Carol

What I appreciated most from Mom and Dad and the Bank of Carol setup was that Mom and Dad never asked me why I wanted my money or what I was planning on spending my money on. If I wanted to withdraw $20, Mom and Dad would promptly hand it over, of course after asking if I wanted a $20 bill or some other denomination.

There were a couple of times as a young elementary school kid where I had fun "testing the system" by withdrawing all of my cash all at once from Mom and Dad. These were usually short-lived experiences where I had fun just holding a pile of cash in my hands or had fun just counting the money out on the carpet. After the novelty wore off within the next hour or so, I usually gave the money back to Mom and Dad "for safekeeping" in the Bank of Carol.

Mom and Dad's method did two things for me:

1) It got me used to monetary transactions before I ever stepped into a financial institution or used an ATM. This was because they asked all the questions a teller would ask: which account I wanted to withdraw from, how much I wanted to withdraw, and what denomination I wanted my money in.

2) Mom and Dad were giving me a form of privacy, the same kind of privacy you give a kid when they're on the phone or in the bathroom. By giving me privacy, it made me feel as though Mom and Dad trusted me, even if they didn't agree with what I spent my money on.

With my explicit trust in the Bank of Carol's prompt transactions, and Mom and Dad's implicit trust in what I did with my money, there was mutual trust in our parent-kid relationship. With this mutual trust, I was more likely to listen to Mom and Dad when they commented about interest in my Bank of Carol CD, or suggested saving the money for, say, an upcoming family vacation instead of the movies this weekend.

Ultimately, this mutual trust strengthened our family bonds. And once again, this was a way for Mom and Dad to build positive experiences with money—and with family—for me.

DOUG
Embracing Financial Independence

While our daughter was improving her math skills with percentages and compounding, we parents were embarking on another life lesson: financial independence.

By the time Carol was nine years old, we parents had saved enough money to quit our jobs and live off our investments. You can read more about that in *The Military Guide to Financial Independence and Retirement* or The Military Guide website, but in this book we're just going to discuss how your financial independence impacts your child.

We human beings are sensitive to the norms imposed upon us by our culture, and one of those norms is the imperative of "setting a good example for my kid." As we approached financial independence we wondered, "What will our daughter think if we're not working? How can we show that we're still productive members of society? How will our new lifestyle prepare her for her working years?"

Everything worked out fine. In fact, our daughter's even more motivated for her own financial independence. She's seen the difference it made in her parents' health and happiness, and she wants that experience too.

Parents, brace yourself for a bit of news: it's not about you. Oh, your kids still care about you and your behavior—and you'll still embarrass them—but they're largely oblivious to your social standing in our society. They care about how they're keeping up with their school peers in their own personal society, but they don't pay attention to your climb of the corporate ladder.

In a kid's view, if your job responsibilities take you away from them too much then they may actually think less of you. Your value is how much time and attention you devote to them, not how many reportables you have at your MegaCorp division or how much you cut last quarter's operating expenses. And when they go out into the world to seek their own careers, the last thing a young adult wants to do is get stuck in their parent's footsteps. They'll blaze their own trails.

Younger kids might not fully understand the idea of retirement. They certainly aren't ready to dive into the details of budgeting and investing, so it's best to stick to the big picture. They'll be happy to know that you'll have more time to spend with them, and they'll want to know that there's still enough money for some fun.

As we parents approached the end of our paychecks, we started talking about our budget. We reassured our daughter that we had enough money to pay for the house, our food, the cars, and the really important part: her allowance. We had enough money to afford everything we needed, and we had a little more money for the things we wanted.

We talked about choices. When our daughter wanted to buy something really expensive we avoided saying "We can't afford it." Instead we'd turn the conversation around to making choices and ask her "How could you afford that?" Could she cut her spending on other things and save more money? Could she spend more time on jobs or would she rather have fun with her friends? How much of her life did she want to work to buy that really nice thing?

A few months after we reached financial independence and I retired, I got a great job offer. I was tremendously flattered by the idea of being paid well to do something that I enjoyed. However, I eventually realized that I'd still have to spend more than 40 hours a week dealing with all the things I didn't enjoy—especially rush-hour commutes.

Our daughter overheard us parents talking about it, and we told her that I'd been offered another teaching job. She knew I liked teaching. We reminded her that we already had enough money in the budget, and we didn't need more. I'd also have to do the new job for at least a year to be fair to the other teachers. The really good news was that, if I accepted the job, we'd have enough extra money from the job for our family to buy a pony.

She was already learning how to ride horses, and she really liked the idea of owning a pony. Everybody wins! She said I should take the job.

We explained that if Mom and I had jobs, then Carol would have less time with us. We'd have to work until almost dinnertime during every school day. We wouldn't be home for her, so she'd have to stay at the after-school program for a few hours. We might even have homework once in a while, or we'd have to travel for work. We wouldn't have as much time to coach her sports team or to help chaperone a school field trip.

Not only would she have less time with her parents, but she'd be responsible for taking care of a pony. It's a big job and she'd have to scoop a lot of pony poop. She was already very familiar with that part of riding a pony.

Once we explained how my job would affect her life, she decided that she'd rather spend more time with us than taking care of a pony. (Whew!) She knew that we already had enough money in the budget, and she said I should skip the job.

Another successful teachable moment.

CAROL
Affording Anything, Not Everything

When talking about Dad's job and pony poop, I learned a valuable lesson: affording anything, not everything. The "One Special Thing" concept was the first time I learned this lesson, but mainly because it was "a rule" and I knew "bad things happened" when I broke the rules. Now with the discussion of Dad's job, I implicitly learned about how money was used to afford all kinds of stuff, and also all kinds of "experiences"—like the freedom of retirement—but money may not be so plentiful as to afford everything.

This was when the power of choice first became visible on a large scale to me. Sure, it would be screaming obvious how important choices were during the Great Recession a few years later, but by listening to Dad talk about "free time" (being at home for me) versus "things" (a pony) I learned this lesson at my own pace, and without the (in)convenience of an economic crash.

Now that I recognized the power of choice, I became more responsible with my choices. Now that I recognized that choices were based on consequences, not "made-up" rules, I would make my choices by weighing what I could achieve in addition to what I desired. Now I understood the concept of a goal. I took into account the consequences, or risks, that would be involved in my choice. Granted, I was still a kid, so my goals were more like "buy a GameBoy Color" and my risks were more like "my GameBoy breaking if I dropped it on the sidewalk." But kids have to start somewhere.

Having an understanding of concepts like risk and goals and the consequences of choice became incredibly important when Mom and Dad started me on one of the next big money topics: types of long-term savings and investments.

SUMMARY
School Opens Up New Opportunities. Be Ready To Use Them!

As kids make new friends (and experience new peer pressure), you'll have more opportunities to talk about shopping and buying. As they learn more math skills you'll have a chance to show them how to count money, make change, and handle their own retail transactions.

You'll have plenty of opportunities to take kids shopping. Here we recommend taking your kids shopping at thrift stores and garage sales instead of more expensive department stores. Help your kids understand cost comparison, such as how much a t-shirt costs second-hand at a thrift store versus brand-new at the brand-name store.

It's also your opportunity to offer incentives for saving money and to show them how compounding works. Start establishing trust in the Bank of Your Kid, complete with withdrawals on demand and giving your kid privacy.

And finally, help your kids understand risks, goals, and consequences of their actions. Remind them of different ways they can spend their money and the long term consequences/rewards instead of purchasing the first gimmie they see.

CHAPTER GOALS

- Teach how to spend small amounts of money and count change.
- Show how savings can compound in a CD.
- Talk about managing money during small daily teachable moments.

CHAPTER FIVE

Tweens and Financial Motivation

> **"**
>
> THERE'S NORMAL, AND
> THEN THERE'S NORDMAN.
>
> **JEFF MOTICHKA**
> ONE OF CAROL'S NAVY BOSSES

**FINANCIAL TERMS AND CONCEPTS
IN THIS CHAPTER**

- Profit-sharing incentives.
- The Kid 401(k).
- The first savings and checking accounts (at banks or credit unions).
- Investing in the stock market.

DOUG
Helping Your Child Build Those Financial Incentives

Our daughter's eighth birthday was a big financial change.

The incentives that we'll describe in this chapter seemed like a good idea to us parents at the time, but years later we started hearing feedback about how unusual they really were. Jeff Motichka, one of Carol's Navy bosses, summed it up quite succinctly in his epigraph comment about her way of creating incentives.

These ideas shouldn't be unusual. We're going to turn these novel Nordman financial incentives into a new normal.

By the third grade, our daughter was a school expert. She knew all the rules (and followed most of them). She absolutely loved school supplies (and still does). She understood how to pay for lunch, and field trips taught her all about school buses.

All of those parts of her life became more teachable moments with more opportunities for financial motivation.

It started with school supplies. Savvy parents learn to shop for them all year long (especially at thrift stores and garage sales) instead of waiting for the back-to-school list and Amazon Prime Day. If our daughter helped with the perpetual school-supplies scavenger hunt, then she got to keep half of the savings.

This was the beginning of the "profit sharing" concept: if our daughter found a cheaper way to buy something, she received her share of the benefits.

Next we gave her an incentive for school lunch. Each week that we handed over the lunch money, she could decide whether to spend it all on school food or, if she brought a (healthy) lunch from home, she could keep half of the lunch money she didn't spend. As she got older, the schools upgraded from paper lunch tickets to electronic debit cards. We upgraded her planning skills by giving Carol her lunch money monthly, and eventually by semester. We also helped her figure out a budget to keep track of how much money she was spending on lunch—as well as how much she was saving by bringing a home lunch.

By elementary school Carol was also a grocery-store expert who could load a cart and check off a list. (She still needed help reaching the high shelves, but she was growing fast.) During each trip we'd talk about the prices of school lunch, the grocery store's prepared lunches, and the home lunch. Buying a packaged lunch from the grocery store could be the One Special Thing (see Chapter 2), but we were also big coupon shoppers. If she clipped coupons for the items on our grocery list (not just junk snacks!) then she got to keep half of the savings.

We even offered transportation incentives. We gave her the money to take the bus to middle school, but if she rode her bicycle then she got to keep half of what we saved. However if she overslept and we had to drive her to school to beat the tardy bell, then she had to pay us extra for the ride. It was amazing how the threat of that "penalty" kept her moving in the mornings.

Carol also took an initiative we never dreamed of. She figured out that if she could finish all of her homework during the breaks throughout the day, then she didn't have anything heavy to carry home. On those days, she called us (back then she had to use the school's front office phone) to let us know she was walking home. A couple of hours later (right on time!) she would be home. We gave her half the savings from not taking the bus.

CAROL
Bicycling

Bicycling is a popular concept in the FIRE (Financial Independence/ Retire Early) community because it's a very cheap alternative to cars. The Nordman family independently developed riding bicycles as a time- and money-saving measure thanks to ridiculous local traffic. Dad had figured out early on that he could save time, gas, and car maintenance money, and even reduce his stress and improve his health by cycling to work every day.

Remember how kids see everything? I saw Dad riding his bike to and from work every day, and I was motivated to learn how to cycle myself. Unlike driving, there was no legal age for biking. Mom and Dad did not drive me anywhere—to school, to the local hangouts, or to after-school activities within biking distance—except for paid after-school activities that were too far to walk or bike. And biking was MUCH faster than walking and less sweaty than running.

Dad didn't just teach me how to ride a bike. He also made sure that I could use hand signals and followed the rules of the road and traffic crossings. Dad took the time to get the right size helmet and safety vest for me. He also taught me basic bicycle maintenance, like replacing a tire and greasing the gears. From Kindergarten into third grade, Dad also biked to and from school with me. By the time I was in fourth grade, he trusted my skills and let me bicycle to school on my own from then on.

Like many things I owned, my bicycle was my responsibility growing up. I had to take care of my bicycle, and I had to keep track of it (for example, I had to remember if I left my bike at a friend's house). I was always welcome to ask for help, or to choose to "upgrade" with my own money, but ultimately my bike was my choice and my money took care of it. These skills as a child quickly translated into taking care of cars as an adult.

CAROL
Incentives For Grades

A common tactic some of my classmates grew up with was getting money for good grades—typically Bs or better—at the end of every quarter. This tactic may work for your own kids. A word of caution: this incentive does not accurately represent the salaried "real world."

One of the other things my peers and I have figured out—military and non-military—is that the reward for finishing efficiently and with quality is...more work. A lot of us struggled with doing "good work" for the first couple of years in the adult world as we tried to strike a balance between "doing everything" and "working too hard."

Instead of using money to reward good grades, I recommend using *privileges* to reward good grades. This could mean staying up an hour later on the weekends, getting to order a custom pizza a couple nights a month on Mom and Dad's dime, or getting a free ride to the mall this Saturday instead of having to walk. Choosing what rewards to give depends on the kid, and you as the parent will recognize which ones suit your kids best. After all, in the real world, it seems like the best employees get the best "preference" and "privilege," even if they're not making the most money.

DOUG
Family Meetings And New Privileges

I should explain the groundwork that led to our daughter's next big financial incentive.

When Carol reached preschool age, she joined our family meetings. Marge and I routinely set aside a few minutes every day to review schedules or to coordinate our parenting tactics. Now Carol sat with us every few weeks for the big discussions. We'd bring up major events like moving to a new military duty station or planning a vacation. Other times we'd discuss house rules or raise Carol's allowance. We kept the meetings to 5-10 minutes for Carol's attention span, and we always asked her to share her feelings or her opinions.

Every family can use upcoming birthdays as milestones for new privileges. During your parenting discussions and family meetings, think about what new things your kid wants to do (riding their bike to the local park by themselves) and what you'd agree to (only on weekend afternoons). Keep the family meetings short and fun, and give everyone a little room to negotiate. Agree to reasonable requests immediately, while bigger ones might have limits of "once a week" or "after chores are done." If you're "going to think about it," then let them know when a decision will come. Kids want good rules and clarity in their negotiations, just like grownups want them in the workplace.

As kids get older, they can handle more responsibility along with a little more freedom. What does success or failure look like for their next milestone privilege? What do you parents need your kid to understand before you can say "Yes!" to their ideas?

These meetings are a great time to announce new financial incentives that will kick in at their next birthday! If you're going to raise their allowance then you can add more financial responsibility, too, like having to save a portion of the higher amount or donate more to charity. Maybe they'll do more chores. Maybe you'll pay a higher rate for a job, but you'll also expect a higher quality of work and you'll teach them a new skill to go with that new job.

They're not just looking forward to gifts and a party, but also to being treated more like a big kid or even a grownup. It's a rite of passage.

You can also take deferred gratification to a new level by setting new financial goals. One day when my spouse and I were talking about our retirement accounts, we realized that we could help our daughter learn about them too. That turned into a parenting discussion about gigantic financial goals like saving for years and watching investments grow from years of compounding, not just from contributions. What huge milestone does every young kid want for their own independence?

That parental brainstorming led to our biggest financial incentive— and our best family meeting ever.

DOUG
The Kid 401(k)

As we mentioned in Chapter 1, kids think that adults are crazy about the mysterious "college fund." Kids get money as birthday gifts, but then parents make kids lock that lovely cash into a savings account that they can't touch for at least TEN YEARS. To a kid, that's an entire lifetime!

We parents remembered what that felt like. We decided to set a more reasonable goal from our own teen experiences: the car fund.

First we announced to Carol that we were going to raise her allowance for her eighth birthday. She was a year older and responsible enough to manage more money. ("Yay!") Then we told her that we were raising her allowance an extra $5/week, but she'd have to deduct $3/week and invest it into a 401(k). "Hunh?"

Then we explained that grownups had to save our money in 401(k)s to achieve financial independence. Grownups had 401(k)s with their jobs, where they saved part of their paychecks to get ready for retirement. Retirement could be a long time and could require a lot of money. Carol knew what retirement was because her grandparents had been retired for years by her eighth birthday.

Best of all, 401(k)s have employer matching. For every extra dollar of her allowance that went into the Kid 401(k), she'd get matching dollars from Mom and Dad. We'd put all of the money into investments and help her watch it grow. Investments might even grow faster than her Bank of Carol CDs.

The catch was that she couldn't touch the money until she was 16 years old. The good news was that she'd have her driver's license, and she could buy her own car!

It blew her mind to realize that someday she'd be 16 years old, and she'd have a car just like Mom and Dad.

Back in the year 2000, it seemed reasonable to tell an eight-year-old that her Kid 401(k) would grow to $5,000 by her 16th birthday. She'd have enough money to buy an older used car with a few dollars left over for gas and insurance.

Behind the scenes, we did the spreadsheet math on the Kid 401(k) to make $5/week (with matching) turn into $5,000 in eight years. We used a very generous match (see Appendix A) and the investments grew at 1% per month. (We could discuss reasonable stock-market returns some other day. For now, the important goal was to show the miracle of compounding.) We calculated eight years of 401(k) contributions (and matches!) compounding to $5,000 at her 16th birthday. That spreadsheet showed her current 401(k) balance whenever she reviewed her budget and her Bank of Carol CDs.

You can use the table in Appendix A at the back of this book, or you could build your own spreadsheet for a different amount.

The Kid 401(k) was also a great way to make plans. We could discuss what type of car she'd like to drive, how to budget for its gas and maintenance, and how to find a good used car. She really enjoyed imagining her life as a grownup, and she also showed a new interest in taking care of a car. Of course there were plenty of opportunities to discuss all of these topics while she was earning money washing and waxing our cars.

A few years later the Kid 401(k) paid an unexpected dividend: it gave her the confidence to plan her own financial future instead of Keeping Up With The Joneses.

You parents know that kids are competitive, and as they approach the teen years it can get vicious. During the early 2000s the older kids were watching TV shows like "MTV Cribs" and "Pimp My Ride" with over-the-top homes and cars. The blatant hyperconsumerism was popular with young adults and teens, and it was magical for middle-school kids.

After our daughter had a few years in her Kid 401(k) plan, one day the 12-year-olds were talking trash amongst themselves about their teen driving aspirations. I was the invisible parent on the sidelines, quietly eavesdropping on their conversation while pretending to read my book:

Kid #1: "Did you see Pimp My Ride? When I'm 16 years old and get my driver's license, my Mom and Dad are buying me a Mustang GT!"

Kid #2: "Really? When I'm 16 years old and get my driver's license, my parents are going to buy me an Escalade!"

Kid #3: "Yeah? When I'm 16 years old my parents are going to buy me a Hummer!"

Carol: "When I'm 16 years old, my Kid 401(k) will have $5,000 in it, and I'm going to buy my own car and gas and insurance!"

(Silence.)

Kid #2: "What's a Kid 401(k)?"

The idea caught on quickly. A couple weeks later the other kids' parents asked us about the Kid 401(k).

In Chapter 7 we'll talk about what happened with the Kid 401(k). Our daughter blew our parental minds with her own creativity and initiative.

CAROL
A 401(k) With $5,000 is Better Than the Lottery!

Like all kids believe, I thought the ultimate get-rich-quick scheme was winning the lottery. I dreamt of one day buying a winning lottery ticket. The book *If You Made a Million* by David M. Schwartz had given me plenty of ideas for how to spend that jackpot.

But in true childish fashion, I thought having a Kid 401(k) was better than having a winning lottery ticket, because:

1) Kids can't legally purchase lotto tickets.

2) Lotto tickets cost a whopping $5 apiece at a minimum. I could've spent that on a Jamba Juice smoothie or a movie ticket or a discount DVD or five ice cream cones instead!

3) I've heard of other kid's parents who had been buying lotto tickets for years and still didn't win the jackpot. Who says I'd be any luckier?

Having a Kid 401(k) was like having already won a small lottery prize. With this Kid 401(k), as long as I kept making contributions, I would have $5,000 with my name on it. Even if I didn't see that $5,000 for years, that was still shorter than the "maybe never" of winning a lottery. Besides, I already had some spending cash: the remainder of my allowance that I could freely spend and save outside the Kid 401(k). And that was good enough for me!

To be honest, I don't remember that conversation with my fellow 12-year-olds. What I remember more in middle school was that my money knowledge was another thing that made me "not normal." It was around my middle school years that I started "filtering" how I talked about money. Like the Kid 401(k) example above, I was already light years ahead of my peers when it came to understanding money, and sometimes this led to confusion or a misunderstanding that ultimately led to either:

1) Kids wanting me to loan money to them, or

2) Kids thinking I'm weird or "so rich" that it set me apart and made me "different."

There were ways I got around these problems. The first was that I never loaned MY money to anyone, including friends. If a friend really really REALLY needed to borrow money, like $5 or $10, I would say "ok, here's $15 and we'll call it your birthday present." That way, I didn't have to remember getting money back, and I didn't have to buy a present for my friend's birthday. The second was that I stopped talking about money, and only talked about it when I was asked a direct question or if it was part of schoolwork.

I've always been a bigger, taller person, so no one ever tried to steal my lunch money or rob me of my wallet. I still took precautionary measures. When in elementary school, I left my wallet at home most days, and only brought in money on book fair days. When in middle school, I kept at most $20 on me, but kept the rest of my cash at home. I planned ahead for big purchases, and I would load the extra cash in my wallet when I was ready to spend.

If bullies stealing money is a challenge for your kid, consider setting up a system that prevents them from having their money stolen. As Dad mentioned earlier, I would receive a semester's worth of lunch money at a time, and would deposit the money in my school's lunch account as soon as possible, during the school's "registration days." Usually on the first day of the new quarter or semester, teachers know kids have checks and wads of cash to deposit in their school lunch accounts, and are quick to help kids get their money deposited

A gift for you

Take what works for you and leave the rest. From JC Webber III

before bullies start hunting. I also remember my high school had a cashier set up separately from the meal lines, so that students could walk up during any meal and deposit money in their account. On those days, I would deposit my money during the "morning recess" meal (which I didn't eat) to get the money out of my hands as quick as possible.

DOUG
The First Checking Account

Our daughter's life changed yet again at age nine: our credit union let her open a checking account.

They even gave her an ATM card! She already knew how to use one, and she was thrilled to be able to get her own money out of the machine, with a card that had her name on it.

A couple of weeks later she lost the ATM card. (She never found it.) Back then the card was only good for a year, but the real sting of this disaster was that the credit union charged $25 for replacing a lost card. We parents waited to see what she'd decide to do. Her frugal habits came through: she lived without that card for the rest of the year until it expired and the credit union sent her a new one. In the meantime, she relied on us parents to make cash withdrawals, but would sometimes have to wait for us parents to make our own ATM trips. Those waits reminded Carol of how important it was to keep track of your ATM card.

CAROL
Losing The First ATM Card

That was a long rest of the year. It's been decades since then and I still remember the pain of losing that card! But since then, I've never lost a credit card, I.D. card, or other important card. With 20/20 hindsight, this was a cheap way for me to learn a very valuable lesson!

DOUG
Using the First Checking Account

The checking account began as a tremendously stressful experience. It forced a fourth-grader to track her checks in the checkbook register, to write neatly, and to do the math correctly. (Math wasn't just for good grades anymore!) She learned (the hard way) to record the checks as soon as she wrote them. She certainly learned how frustrating it can be to take your time and figure out your mistakes, no matter how many times you have to work the numbers.

For the first few months one of us parents helped her go through her statements and balance the checkbook. (Messy writing and bad math caused a few tears, and Carol wasn't very happy about it either.) A month or two later we showed her how to enter her transactions into Quicken, and it became much easier for her to reconcile the register.

The best part about the checkbook was that it helped her feel like a grownup. We started electronically transferring all of her allowances and other funds (the same way grownups are paid!) and tried to stop using cash. When the school was registering for programs or holding book fairs, she could whip out her checkbook and pay for her purchases. (She really enjoyed the looks on her teachers' faces. By the end of those events, every teacher had heard about our daughter.) When she had to pay for horse riding lessons or taekwondo, she could write out her own checks for the coaches.

With great power, however, comes great responsibility—even when you're nine years old.

One day as we were making the long drive home from a riding lesson, we realized that she'd forgotten to pay the coach. It was no big deal to our daughter, because she thought that she'd just write a bigger check next week. The coach was too polite to say anything, but we parents knew how it felt to be stiffed out of a paycheck.

It was another teachable moment, although the timing was terrible: even though it was a 30 minute drive to the ranch, we turned the car around and headed back. Along the way, we talked about how our daughter would feel if we forgot to transfer her weekly allowance. ("We'd make it up next week, right?") We talked about the coach's budget and paying her rent and her electric bill, and how she even had to buy food for her dog. It was a big epiphany for a kid: her checkbook kept the economy moving. She realized that even if her sports money was given to her for free, it made a big difference in the coach's life.

When we got to the ranch, we waited in the car while she wrote out the check and then ran it over to the coach. She never forgot another payment.

As she used up her checks and had to order new ones, she learned another valuable life lesson about marketing. The check company's website let her order all sorts of cool layouts and pictures, and she designed the world's most beautiful personalized checks... only to realize that she'd have to spend several months of her allowance for the extra fees. (Or she'd have to get a really good job!) She reluctantly decided that she'd rather have the money for other things in her budget, and the basic (boring) check design was good enough.

I have to admit that we parents weren't sure how her choice was going to work out. She really enjoyed showing off her checkbook to teachers and other kids, and those fancy checks would have been major bonus points with the cool crowd.

Since her school days in the early 2000s, of course, paper checks have practically disappeared. Ironically, a few years after our daughter learned how to balance her checkbook, we parents stopped balancing ours. If we were raising a child in the third millennium, we would have skipped the checkbook phase and gone straight to debit cards. In the next chapter we'll mention more ways to handle family debit cards.

If we were raising our daughter today then she'd also track her finances on a smartphone, but that's another story, too.

 CAROL
Freedom And Privacy: Steps To Maturity

Dad's comment about "Never forgot another payment" stretches into the present. I've never missed a payment on a credit card or other service. Another cheap way to learn a life-long lesson!

Although Mom and Dad made sure I never asked them for money for entertainment (not even $20 for the movie theater as a teen), I still felt somewhat tethered to them money-wise because I couldn't get cash without their assistance. Thanks to all the teachable moments over the years, I'd seen my parents drop off checks at banks for cash, or make withdrawals from ATMs. But I couldn't do that myself until I had my own checking account.

Once I had my own bank account, I could get my OWN cash from my OWN bank account to fill my OWN wallet whenever I-I-I-I-I wanted. All I had to do was keep the balance above $0.00.

Now I could go to the movies whenever I had enough cash to do so. Now I could buy ice cream or soda at school whenever I had enough cash to do so. I still have some of the books and school supplies I bought at school book fairs with my own checks.

This way, when I got a check on my birthday or Christmas, I didn't have to involve Mom and Dad anymore. In the past, I would oogle at the check amount to my heart's content, then promptly hand the check over to Dad for "depositing" (which often included taking the check to the ATM with Dad to deposit in HIS account). But now, that check would be deposited in MY account, AND I could choose right away what happened next with that check. I could choose to save that money in my Savings Account (and transfer it right there on the ATM or on our home computer), or contribute to my Kid 401(k) (a simple transfer to Dad's account, also right there on the ATM or on our home computer), or I could cash out and finally buy that Game Boy Color I'd been talking about buying for the last six months.

It was a real taste of true freedom!

But how do you keep a kid from overdrawing the account? For me, it was simple logic: if I overdrew my account, I would then owe a $25 overdraft fee. Though I didn't know how, I knew that somehow Mom and Dad would find out (because they seem to find out EV-'RY-THING), and that I'd somehow get in trouble for overdrawing. And after I finished my punishment for overdrawing (no TV or whatever it would be this time), I'd still owe $25 to the bank for overdrawing the account, which was more than a month's allowance. That was enough to keep me in line.

Now I could make decisions on WHEN I was going to withdraw my money, or WHEN I was going to deposit money, or WHEN I was going to save money. And again, I could make these decisions independently from Mom and Dad, though I knew they were always there to offer coaching if I asked for it.

Mom and Dad would supervise me, but they also respected my privacy. They never "snooped" on my accounts or told me the state of my funds. They didn't try to open my statements behind my back or pass judgement on whether or not they thought I was managing my money well. This meant that I had plenty of space to "scorch my fingers" without causing serious damage.

For example, I learned the importance of using my own bank's ATMs. Because I was a kid with a no-frills checking account, I once had to pay a $3 ATM fee on the $20 I withdrew from a "convenience" ATM at a different bank in the neighborhood. When I noticed the transaction on my bank statement, I asked Dad about it and why it was there. Dad then explained it to me matter-of-factly, and refrained from lecturing me on why I shouldn't waste my money on ATM fees. By giving me this information without judgement AND with the "space" to make my own decision, I decided that I didn't like paying ATM fees on my own. I also came up with my own solution to avoid the fee: since my family also went to our bank's ATM every Sunday en route to the grocery store, I planned my cash flow around going to the ATM on Sunday. It wasn't long before "planning my cash" turned into "budgeting my allowance."

Although checkbook balancing isn't used often anymore, it positively affected one of my school grades. In seventh grade I signed up for a home economics class for a purely selfish reason: home ec students got to eat all the cookies they baked in class.

Yes, I signed up for free food. Some things are universal.

But one of the other modules taught in the class was how to manage a home budget, complete with balancing a paper register similar to what I had in my checkbook. On the day the assignment was due, the teacher saw that a classmate's register was wrong because there was a two-cent difference in the balance (where it should've been zero cents), but neither the teacher nor the student could find the mistake. The teacher—who remembered me as the kid who wrote her own registration checks at the beginning of the school term—called me over and asked me to help them find the difference. Five minutes later, I found the error, and the teacher gave me a 10% bonus to my class grade. It was a win-win-win situation for me, the classmate, and the teacher, and it's an event I will never forget!

DOUG
Teaching A Pre-teen About Investing

Like everyone else during the 1990s Internet bull market, I decided that I finally had the online resources to pick stocks. Instead of going to libraries to research Value Line's paper manuals, I could surf the Web from my hotshot 28.8 kbps modem. I'd learned a lot about Warren Buffett over the years, and I wanted to be a brilliant investor, too.

My spouse and I had a steady military income, so we invested aggressively in a portfolio of at least 90% equities. (The rest was in CDs and money markets.) I limited my stock-picking to about 10% of our portfolio, and the rest of our equities were in mutual funds or exchange-traded funds. I tracked my investing performance against the benchmarks.

I wanted to brag, er, I mean, share this knowledge with Carol too, so I started showing her how we could invest in stocks. She was skeptical at first, and wasn't sure about risking her money. I put together a separate list in our Quicken financial software and showed her what her stocks could do if she invested $100. After a while she decided to risk some of her savings in a company we knew all too well: Disney.

It turns out that I was not a brilliant investor. I had to work very hard to match the benchmarks, and by 2007 I'd decided to return to passively-managed index funds with low expense ratios. I was getting 99.9% of the stock market's return for about 1% of the effort.

Carol? Well, she might still be a brilliant investor. Her investing experience had some gains and a few losses. More importantly, though, she learned her investor's tolerance. She learned enough to understand the basics of investing, but she wasn't fascinated by the idea. She seemed to lose interest in picking stocks and she stuck to index funds.

She moved on to more important things in life, like being a teenager.

CAROL
Dipping My Toes Into Investing

At some point around the time I was 10 or 11 years old, Mom and Dad thought I had a handle on my cash and my checkbook. Did they always agree with what I was spending my money on? 99% of the time, the answer was "HECK NO!" But at the same time, they could tell that I was showing maturity by using "longer term" planning methods—buying that Game Boy Color after saving for six months, for example—and that I was probably ready to start talking about other types of longer term planning. The stock market seemed like a good place to start.

At the time that Mom and Dad started figuring out how to turn stock investments into a "teachable moment," they were using online research tools at Fidelity Investments. Although the website has changed over the years, I remember how Dad would casually call me over to our desktop computer when he was looking at his stock portfolio, and he'd show me how much extra money per dollar he was making for investing. Some of the companies he mentioned were meaningless adult…"thingies," but other companies caught my attention, like Disney, Ford Motor Company (our family car was a Ford then), and Nike sportswear.

"Imagine if you could own a little piece of these companies," said Dad. "As these companies make money, so will you. I bet you could guess how many millions of dollars Disney makes when families like ours go to Disneyland or buy a Disney movie. Imagine if you got some money out of every single product Disney sold. That's what the stock market lets people like you—an 'investor'—do. There's one big risk here: no one knows when exactly all of these families are going to buy Disney, or buy something from Universal Studios or DreamWorks instead. So there's a chance that a company like Disney will lose money, and so will you."

I wasn't quite convinced that investing in stocks was what I wanted to do with the little money I had. So Dad made an experiment for me: he invested $100 of his own money in Disney, and let me check up on the stock every week or so to see with my own eyes what happened. It was a bit of a reality check to only see the stock value change by mere dollars and cents at a time, but Dad would pull out an old 1980's-style calculator from his college days[4], and walk me through the profit an investor would get if they bought, say, $1,000 or $10,000 or $100,000 of Disney stock at a time. For a 10-year-old, that was a much bigger number than anything I'd earn in a couple of YEARS, and *that* convinced me that investing in the stock market was a great idea.

---

[4] It's now 2020 and that calculator still works. Talk about tools that last!

91

DOUG
Encouraging Your Child to Read About Money

One of my brilliant parenting ideas turned out to be... not so brilliant after all.

I thought that Carol would enjoy reading books that I'd found useful. After all, I'd only pass on the best one out of at least a dozen, and it would be a book that I thought would help her move toward adulthood.

CAROL
Reading About Money

Dad is an AVID reader. He's the only adult I know that doesn't watch TV, and can read through a stack of a dozen books in about a month or less. Even today, Dad will finish a book and say, "hey Carol, I just finished reading a book called..." and after a brief synopsis, make a casual suggestion that I read it, too. Like any good American child, I probably read about one out of every ten books that Dad suggested.

The same thing happened with money books. Although Dad was passing me books about money since I was old enough to read chapter books, I only ever read a handful of those books. I was simply a kid that found TV and video games far more fascinating. Later, when I was a teenager, I was too busy with schoolwork and after-school jobs to want to read books about money. By the time I was in college and in the military, money books were lower in priority than sleep.

You may also be tempted to hand your kids a book about money instead of having a money conversation. I can personally assure you that your child will never read that book (or this one!). The reality is: your kids are much more likely to listen to you than they are to read a book about money. And if you question if your kids are listening to you in the first place, then they're spending even less time reading about money!

A happy medium is articles and blog posts. When I was younger, articles would come from places like CNBC's money section. As I got older and blogs were more common (hello, Mr. Money Mustache), Dad would start sending me posts from blogs instead. Even today, Dad will send a "weekend links" email to me on the *ahem* weekends about all the cool articles he's read about money in the week. I found the articles easier to digest than 200-something page books. Consider doing the same for your kid.

DOUG
Reading and Teens

As you might imagine, the revelations of Carol's last few paragraphs were a bit of a surprise. (Thanks, honey!) When I passed her those books, I just let her know that I'd be happy to answer questions. I never nagged her about reading them.

After learning about Carol's reading priorities, I did an informal survey of other teens and young adults. Big surprise: today's young adults don't have to read as many books as us Baby Boomers because they're even more efficient at consuming content. Blogs, podcasts, and videos give them even more bite-size choices to browse during rush-hour driving and workouts.

Today, if I wanted to repeat these educational opportunities with a teen, I'd focus on podcasts and blogs. (They've already found the videos.) I still send a "Dad's Weekend Links" email, and I try to limit myself to a handful of links.

But I can tell that she listened and learned from all of our talks during the years.

SUMMARY
Figure Out What Motivates Your Child.

Now that they're old enough to manage their money and go shopping, give your kids more incentives to practice and improve. Find out what sort of privileges motivate your family, and reward their initiatives.

Help your kids learn more about saving and investing. When they're ready, show them how to open a checking account and perhaps get a debit card. Consider your own version of the Kid 401(k) to inspire delayed gratification for a long-term goal. Find out if they're really interested about actively investing in the stock market, or whether they'll prefer a passively-managed index fund. If they have a hard time grasping the concept in a conversation, consider making an experiment by investing a small amount of cash (say, $100), and let your kids watch the money grow.

CHAPTER GOALS

- Give kids a share of the savings for finding coupons for grocery shopping, packing a lunch, and bicycling to school.
- Teach young kids to save and invest for years (their first car).
- Help them open their checking account when they're ready to do the work.
- Show them how to invest in the stock market and help them find their risk tolerance.

CHAPTER SIX

Teens: An Attitude, Not Just An Age

> 66
>
> THE TEENAGE YEARS ARE RIDICULOUSLY CRUCIAL AND HARD AND, UM, AWKWARD.
>
> **AIMEE TEEGARDEN**
> AWARD-WINNING TEEN ACTRESS

**FINANCIAL TERMS AND CONCEPTS
IN THIS CHAPTER**

- Managing larger amounts of money over longer periods of time.
- The "Can I afford it?" question and asking "How can I afford that?"
- The first debit cards and credit cards.
- Wages and taxes for part-time work at the first "real" job.
- Starting a Roth IRA as a teenager.

DOUG
Our Big-Picture Perspective On Parenting A Teen

Teens should make their biggest money mistakes at home with their family—with people they trust and can learn from. Home is better for making mistakes than in college, or, even worse, in the real world when credit scores really matter. Carol and I have heard from many young adults who never learned financial skills while they were growing up. Even worse, too many of them are dealing with tens of thousands of dollars of consumer debt and student loans.

Teens will save their worst behavior (and their harshest words) for the people they love and feel safe with. It's their way of expressing their own character and fluttering their fledgling wings on the edge of the nest as they get ready to start their own lives. Parents still hold the power in the family and shouldn't be offended by these declarations of independence. (I struggled with that part!) You can use those teachable moments to help them build their adult lives.

Teens are also old enough to learn to manage their money in bigger increments, like a monthly allowance instead of weekly.

Another challenge of the teen years is developing their judgment and decision-making skills. Every teen learns this at a different pace, and they all need plenty of practice. Some might figure it out by age 15 (like Carol) while a few (like me) might not develop it until their mid-20s.

We parents kept reminding ourselves of those reassurances as our daughter moved through her teen rites of passage. That part of our lives wasn't always pretty, but we got through it. Today our daughter amazes us with her creativity, persistence, resilience, and accomplishments. And we're not saying that just because she's co-writing this book!

As our daughter entered her teens, she was already an experienced consumer. She had her preferences for food, clothing, and toiletries, and now she was experimenting with everything the American marketing machine was selling. She was also very active in sports, going through tremendous growth spurts, and consuming amazing quantities of groceries.

We could definitely see the results in our household spending. We tried to exploit this phase of her life as yet another opportunity to develop greater financial skills.

Instead of the classic parental tactic of "We can't afford that," we started with "We don't have money in the budget for that. What do you think we should give up to buy that?"

Later on we changed the entire debate by asking "How can we find a way to afford that?" and "What would 'Yes!' look like?" We tried to avoid rationing our money from an attitude of scarcity. Instead the discussion moved to spending more efficiently (and cutting the waste) or earning more money. Our attitude shifted toward abundance: we can afford anything, just not everything. The focus changed from confrontations into discussions about making the numbers work. Instead of a teen arguing with parental authority figures, our daughter was practicing new negotiation skills and solving problems.

If the debate ended without an agreement, though, there was always the parent's ultimatum: *"You're going to have to spend your own money for that."* When the funds had to come out of her own allowance (or out of her own life energy) then we'd all find out whether her spending was truly aligned with her values.

Finally, today there are plenty of board games (and websites) to help kids learn about earning, saving, and spending. Some schools use financial-literacy tools to help kids figure out their money personalities and to teach them the basic skills. One of the fastest-growing school games is Cash Flow Crunch. We've learned about CFC through financial conferences and Doug is friends with the inventors, Paul and Sherene Vasey. They're doing great work across America, and they can help you find more teachable moments with your family.

CAROL
Learning From Suze Orman's "Can I Afford It?" Segments

If a teen doesn't listen to their own parents, who else might they listen to? For me, it was financial guru Suze Orman. By the time I was a teen, Suze Orman's CNBC show was a hit, and Mom was a frequent viewer. While Mom had the patience to listen to Suze's lectures, I only had patience for the game-like "Can I Afford It?" segment.

In "Can I Afford It?," participants would call into the show with a particular desire and why the item was desired; a designer purse, an iPad, a house, jewelry, or a bride's $400 teeth whitening appointment ahead of the wedding, for example. While on-air, Suze Orman and the participant would discuss why the participant wanted the desired item or service, and often Suze would pass her judgement on whether the desire had a logical reasoning behind it and if there was another way to procure the item by spending less money (to the bride's teeth whitening appointment, Suze said something like "I get my teeth white with Crest White Strips, and they're only a fraction of the $400 you want to pay"). Suze would then say, "show me the money," a cue to the participant to disclose their money profile, which included:

- age,
- income (including spouse's income, if applicable),
- expenses (including mortgage),
- debt, and
- savings (including liquid, investment, college savings, and retirement).

She would also ask how the participant planned to pay for the desired item. As the participant verbally listed everything, the amounts were listed on screen next to Suze. As the viewer read through the tally and listened to the participant's background, they could watch Suze's expression. From there, Suze would (eventually) give the participant one of two verdicts: "approved" or "denied." My teenage self thought it was funny that Suze's verdict of "denied" often sounded like "DENIED!!!"

"Can I Afford It?" was a live game for me to size up a participant's savings and their desires, and guess what verdict Suze would give and why. Suze always explained why she approved or denied her participant's desires, so I could compare my answer and logic to hers. Often, Suze would point out why a purchase didn't need to be made at all, even if Suze approved the purchase. This was a fantastic way for me to see dozens of real-world gimmies, some of which were gimmies I had myself (like Apple technology). It was nice to have an expert (who wasn't my parents) advise the participant (who wasn't me), in a manner that I could observe.

The segment also helped me improve my financial negotiations with Mom and Dad. The participants always had a "negotiation" with Suze by explaining "why" they wanted the item to Suze. That explanation would prompt an on-air discussion in which the participant was trying to "get to Yes" with Suze. By watching other people attempt the discussion with Suze Orman, I learned more about what reasonings worked and didn't work, and why. This made me smarter and more efficient in my approach to financial negotiations with Mom and Dad. I think my parents appreciated Suze's teaching.

Nowadays, Suze Orman's "Can I Afford It" segments are on YouTube, so your own children can skip the show and dive right into the game. Will today's participant be approved, or denied, and why?!

DOUG
The Teen Profit-Sharing Challenge

In the teen years, the school supplies budget started a new spending challenge.

During the elementary and middle-school years, most of the supplies were consumables. It seemed that we were perpetually shopping for more paper towels and pencils, and somehow it all got used before the end of the year. We kept an eye out for bargains and stocked up whenever we could.

In high school, the list expanded to include items like special graphing calculators for the advanced math classes. These cool math tools were $75-$100, and for some reason they couldn't be used for the next grade's advanced math class. The TI-84 that worked perfectly well in ninth grade suddenly lacked an important new feature for tenth grade which could only be fulfilled by the TI-89. The teachers implied that if their students wanted to get into a good college, well then, they'd have to use good college tools[5].

These machines were the size of a brick, and they tended to get banged up as they were passed around. At the end of the day they'd be stuffed into a backpack (under heavy textbooks) and thrown around on the way home for more number-crunching. As expensive as the calculators were, the casual neglect and abuse could kill them before the year was out. (The calculators, not their owners.) Why should a teen take care of it anyway? They knew they had to get a different one next year.

The solution: profit-sharing calculators, too.

It turned out that this year's graphing calculator could be sold to next year's students, or even sold online. If the calculator had all of its manuals, cases, and accessories in "like new" condition then it could sell for most of its original price. If our daughter took care of her calculator and sold it at the end of the year then she got to keep half of the revenue, and in cash! Any neglect or damage came out of her share of the sale.

Our profit-sharing incentives finally aligned our student's financial motives with ours.

---

[5] Carol also reports that she didn't use any of her high school calculators in college. By then, it was more important that students had the right computer programming skills. Students also used calculation websites like Wolfram Alpha to check their work in calculus and other advanced math classes.

It was just one more incentive to take care of her tools and to minimize the wasted spending, but it paid big dividends when she started college.

CAROL
The First Independent Craigslist Venture

Remember how Dad mentioned that "teens should make their biggest money mistakes at home with their family?" Sometimes situations that could turn dangerous or into big mistakes should also occur under parental supervision. One such situation was my first time selling a calculator on Craigslist.

We never dream of our children meeting some stranger on a street corner and exchanging some goods for cash. After all, many of us probably went through the Drug Abuse Resistance and Education (D.A.R.E.) classes, right? But the street corner meet-ups are what a lot of Craigslist transactions look like. How can parents ensure that kids recognize a bargain, and recognize when it's just...too sketchy to be worth it? The answer is that parents should supervise—but not make—the kid's transaction.

There was one graphing calculator that I couldn't sell within my own high school, so I decided to sell it on Craigslist instead. Mom was the "Craigslist peruser" of the family, and had read thousands of Craigslist ads before, so I went to her to help set up the "for sale" posting for my calculator. She read the interested buyers' emails over my shoulder when they started pouring into my email inbox, and we decided that the first person that responded—a college student who needed the calculator for her classes—would be the one to meet up with first. So I crafted a reply email suggesting a local McDonald's at about 4:00 pm the next day, and Mom checked my work one more time before I clicked the Send button. Within 20 minutes, I got an email back from the interested buyer accepting the meet up. In this whole phase of the transaction, Mom had merely supervised while I did all the work.

Remember how when I was first buying ice cream cones as a little kid, Mom would sit at a nearby table during the transaction? The same thing happened when I went to sell my calculator at McDonald's the next day. This time, Dad sat himself at a table within earshot of me, while I approached the interested buyer. The buyer tested the calculator, and agreed to buy it on the spot. I counted the cash with my own hands and in front of her before she departed, and gave her a firm handshake and a thank you like my parents had taught me. Best of all, the whole situation happened under Dad's watchful eye.

Had Dad sensed something amiss, he could've either stepped in to help, or extracted me from the situation with an excuse, and got me out of the transaction before it got dangerous. Had the buyer tried to steal the calculator from me, or short change me, Dad was there to back me up. Having Dad "watching my back" also gave me confidence that I could do this by myself, but had backup within earshot just in case. I think Dad was also reassured that if something happened to his teen, he would be there to help her out.

You may think that your teen will only have to re-sell their expensive calculators a few times, but these are the same skills necessary to maintain and resell any high-priced good. While teens are concerned about calculators and other electronic devices, today's adults hold similar concerns about cars and houses, for example. These lessons served me in the moment as a teen, but have come up again and again as an adult.

DOUG
Negotiating A New Allowance

We also added a new type of allowance: "clothing and cosmetics." As a side benefit, it prevented many arguments.

We parents figured out roughly how much of our spending was going to her clothing, soaps, shampoos, and other "potions." We gave her that lump sum of money each quarter, and eventually stretched it to six-month increments each January and July.

From then on she was in charge of her own clothing and cosmetics. We joked that she could either dress really well or smell really good, but not both. What she spent that money on was her choice. Best of all, that special allowance seemed to avoid the inevitable fashion debates about buying the latest trends. She could experiment with shampoos or accessories or clothing styles whenever she wanted. Anything above the allowance was her problem to solve by saving her own money or doing more jobs around the neighborhood.

The timing of the six-month allowance (at the start of the year and the start of summer) was especially challenging. She could buy expensive items during back-to-school shopping, but that sum also had to stretch through the holidays. Even when she was shopping and making decisions for next week, she also had to forecast her spending through the next six months.

In retrospect, we parents should have sponsored more shopping tours through expensive retail fashion stores. We wouldn't have bought anything, but we could have compared prices (and marketing tactics) to thrift stores and garage sales. This would have given her a better perspective on cost versus value and helped her make more thoughtful choices. More importantly, it would have helped her resist peer pressure from college "friends" and other young adults.

CAROL
Brand Names And Peer Pressure

I knew the expression "keeping up with the Joneses" thanks to the financial education my parents gave me. Academically speaking, I understood how dumb it was to keep up with the Joneses, since it was a great way to waste money and would likely lead to unhappiness.

But in reality, there were many times in elementary school and middle school when I attempted to keep up with the Jone--I mean, "caved in to peer pressure." Some of the things I'd bought under peer pressure definitely did not bring me happiness, like a placemat (that's a long story for another time) or a deck of collectible Yu-Gi-Oh! cards or a video game everyone else was playing that spring break. I still remember the regret of spending my hard-earned money on these purchases. My skills at managing my money and resisting peer pressure were interrelated, and both improved as I got older and gained more experience with spending money.

Managing my own six-month clothing and cosmetic allowance was the ultimate test, money-wise, of resisting peer pressure. By the time I was a teen, the trendy clothes to wear were brands like Hollister, Abercrombie and Fitch, American Eagle, Pac Sun, Billabong, Dakine, and a host of other skate and surf brands. At $40 per t-shirt and as much as $150 per pair of jeans or shirts or a skirt, all of these items were way out of my budget; buying brand-name clothes for one day's wear would cost at least three months' allowance, and that didn't include any soaps, shampoos, or underwear, etc.

And then there were accessories to the outfits. Besides the clothes, teens at my school were also wearing collectable sneakers ($100 and up), fashionable "Lids" (baseball caps at $50 and up) and designer backpacks and/or purses (who knew how many hundreds of dollars those cost). At the time, fancy electronics included RAZR phones (at least a couple hundred dollars) and iPod Videos (a few hundred dollars). All of these accessories were worth months of my budget, too.

So I stuck to a simple clothes formula. I bought thrift-store shorts and t-shirts that would minimize sweating at my open-air, un-air conditioned high school in Hawaii's tropical climate. I wore sneakers that could withstand the dirty outdoor walkways between my classes. Socks and underwear came from the local WalMart. My family's favorite yogurt brand once had an odd rewards program; after mailing in the required number of single-serving yogurt container tops, I got a free red backpack that was perfect for school books and papers. Hats and electronics were not allowed in class (but they could be in your backpack), so I didn't have either with me at school.

In high school, when peers were bored, I was sometimes teased for the way I was dressed, but I was never bullied. I was probably judged behind my back for my style of dress, but it didn't prevent me from having friends or getting good grades or maintaining a busy and positive social life. Some of my friends would offer "makeovers" for me, but I always politely declined. With 20/20 hindsight, each teen was so self-absorbed in his or her own problems that it didn't really matter what I wore. All of us wanted the same thing: to graduate and get the heck out of high school!

DOUG
The First Credit Card

Our daughter also kicked off this important decade with a critical life skill: her first credit card.

Back then the best option was to add her as an authorized user to a parent's card. We ended up applying for a new card because none of our card companies at the time were willing to have a 13-year-old as an authorized user. We also started with a relatively low credit limit (a few hundred dollars) in case there were problems with theft or fraud. We were pretty sure our daughter would be responsible about using the card, but we wanted to avoid setting us up for a thousand-dollar catastrophe.

By now you're probably expecting to read about more drama and disasters. When we look back at those years, we only remember one credit card problem! As far as we can tell, most of the time it sat in her wallet without being used for more than an occasional store purchase. Once in a while we helped her talk with a customer service representative for billing questions.

Back then we didn't use debit cards, but today there are great family tools based on them. One of our favorites is the FamZoo system where the parents can set up their kids' debit cards and control their spending limits. (Disclosure: Doug knows the founder, Bill Dwight.) FamZoo is a family banking system that (for a monthly fee) automates allowances, Bank of Kid CDs, paying for jobs, and even spending limits. We replicated a lot of that with cash and transfers through our credit union's website accounts, but FamZoo has a parent dashboard and many more features. It's one example of how fintech tools make life easier for the parents, not just the kids.

More importantly, a family debit-card system makes it easier to limit the risks of merchant fraud and skimmers. If a service like FamZoo had been around in 2001, we would have happily paid the monthly fee for the tools.

Another issue that cards brought into Carol's financial life, though, was time management. Every teen struggles with staying organized.

She was pretty good at handling homework and studying and projects with her routine of "20 minutes a day," but the monthly chores started to get messy.

We used to joke about "Money Day": the fabled perfect calendar date to handle money chores. Ideally she'd have all of her statements from the credit union and the card company, along with all of her receipts. Her Quicken check register would already have all of her transactions entered. She'd be able to reconcile all of her checks and balance her checkbook (on the first attempt!). Then she'd be able to match all of her charge receipts and schedule her credit-card payment on the card company's website. She'd update all of her spending categories and make sure that she was on track in every part of her budget—and get it all done before lunch.

Of course the reality was a little different. The first hour of her personal Money Day was usually spent finding all of her receipts and trying to organize the paper piles. By this point she had four years of experience with checks and registers, and she knew that she could figure out any mistakes. She'd eventually sort out all of the paper and catch up on the automatic payments. As parents, we'd learned to steer clear of the grumbling until she came to us with a question or a request for help. After several months of learning by experience, she figured out a system that worked for her and she got back on track. Best of all, she created her own system.

In retrospect, I'm really glad that she didn't get her first credit card (or debit card) as a college freshman. She was able to make all of her checking and credit-card mistakes at home, and she learned how to handle everything without the added stress of campus life.

CAROL
Turning Money Day Into
A Weekly Routine

As Dad mentioned above, it took me some time to turn Money Day into something resembling a 20 minutes-a-day habit. The system that finally worked for me was in two parts: having a daily "receipt dump" envelope, and having a weekly "cash plan" in place for every Sunday, when the family took our weekly trip to the bank's ATM ahead of the grocery store. At the end of every day, when I came home, took off my shoes, and stashed my stuff in my room, I took an extra moment to empty the spare change out of my wallet into my Hideaway bank, and then I dumped my receipts in the envelope. Every Sunday morning, before we went to the ATM, I would grab my envelope of receipts, log into my credit card account and bank account, and ensure everything matched with my weekly pile of receipts and my own electronic checkbook record. By having everything matched up before the ATM and grocery store visit, I knew whether or not I needed to make a cash withdrawal from the ATM, and I knew if I had enough room on my credit card and in my budget to buy cosmetics or whatever else I wanted at the grocery store. Money Day went from a monthly event to a weekly event, and shortened from 1-2 hours in one session to 10 minutes a week.

All of that being said, I still made what I consider a major screw-up: The Carol Nordman Bailout of 2009. That was the one time that my parents had to bail me out of my own credit card, at the same time the United States government was bailing several large companies out of their own financial woes. I'm still embarrassed by my "bailout," and I learned a lot from the situation.

As the news cycles reported on government bailouts, I realized that I'd over-spent on my credit card by about $150. I don't even remember what it was or how I'd missed the transaction(s), but I can say for sure that it was my own darn fault for spending more money than I had in my checking account, even with all the profit-sharing and reimbursement deals Mom, Dad, and I had going. One Sunday in 2009, I realized my spending error, and immediately called a family meeting to confess my mistake.

Naturally, Mom and Dad were disappointed in me. Here I was, a senior in high school who had just turned 17 years old, making one of the most basic mistakes of money that my parents had taught me how to avoid for years. Here I was, with an after school job and a healthy allowance, asking for my parents' forgiveness and help in "making ends meet " on my looming credit card bill. Though I'd made a very stupid mistake, I was so embarrassed by it that I was ready to own up to it before it got any worse or took any longer to resolve. I wanted to get it over with as soon as possible.

Mom, Dad, and I agreed that I needed to pay the balance in full to ensure our credit history was unblemished by this mistake. After a few minutes of negotiations, I agreed to complete a list of usually-paid jobs around the house to make up for my "debt." In exchange for the promise, Dad would immediately transfer the money I needed for my bill, and I would immediately pay the credit card bill in full. It would take me another week of doing extra yard work and repairs around the house before I was "even" again.

Mom and Dad could have acted like a credit card company by having me take out a Bank of Carol loan of $150 at some interest rate (8%?) to pay off the credit card. When I asked my parents why they didn't do that, they said that... well... the thought didn't occur to them at the time. This was the first and only time I overspent my credit card, which I self-reported as soon as I had discovered it. Had I overspent my credit card *again* (a clear indication that I did *not* learn my lesson the first time) then maybe Mom and Dad would've had me take out a Bank of Carol loan.

I could've waited for my next after-school paycheck to pay off the debt. A couple of things kept me from doing so: one, that check was already earmarked for deposit into my Roth IRA; two, part of the terms of the bailout was that I had to pay off the debt as soon as possible. This was Mom and Dad's way of illustrating what guru Dave Ramsey calls "a debt emergency," without sacrificing my retirement savings.

The other thing Mom and Dad did was set a six-month "probationary period" on an additional punishment. I was spared any traditional punishment (loss of TV privileges, loss of driving privileges, loss of profit sharing or other financial privileges), but if I messed up again over the next six months, then I would immediately have to serve the "suspended" punishment plus whatever additional punishment I would earn in the second infraction.

Mom and Dad can't take credit for inventing the six-month probationary period idea. The tactic is a common one used in the U.S. military.

I made it through my probationary period without making another mistake, and was relieved when I no longer had the probation "hovering over my head." Not only did I pay closer attention to my spending habits, and really stick to my receipt dump and cash plan habits, but I started keeping a "mini emergency fund" of $200 set aside in each account to prevent ever having to go to Mom and Dad for money ever again. I still keep a "mini emergency fund" of $200 in all of my accounts to this day to prevent another bailout embarrassment.

Teens will test their limits (and yours). That extra $150 may not seem like a lot to you as a parent, but to a teen it is a huge amount. It is better for them to feel the sting of that credit card balance as a teenager with a $150 mistake rather than as a young adult with a mistake costing thousands of dollars.

DOUG
Carol's First REAL Job

Carol's 14th birthday present to herself was another financial leap forward: the state work permit.

For the last seven years, she'd been a math student at our local Kumon tutoring franchise. The curriculum had taught her a lot and helped her learn to handle test anxiety. It also helped her develop a tremendous work ethic: she had to do the Kumon worksheets every day at home, as well as show up at the Kumon center every Wednesday afternoon and Saturday morning.

The local franchise owner employed a half-dozen teens to help run the program with the younger kids. Carol had watched these teens for half of her life and really wanted to emulate their example. The franchise owner had dropped many hints that Carol would be welcome to join the payroll when she turned 14 years old.

That first job had important life lessons, and the first lesson was that homework has priority over work hours. The second lesson was that she'd have more money than ever before passing through her hands, and she should develop a budget for more saving as well as spending. Finally, there was the shock at seeing how much of her wages were going to taxes.

We're not at liberty to discuss the salaries of a Kumon franchise, but it started at the state's minimum wage and quickly rose to Carol's skill level. She worked there part-time for over three years until she started college and she even dropped by to work for a few hours during college vacations.

CAROL
The Early W-2 Income

Having a "real" W-2 income was bittersweet. On the one hand, making $6.75 an hour meant I had just slightly more money coming in from my after-school job than I ever had from my allowance. On the other hand, that slight margin (and then some) was lost to taxes for the first time in my life; Mom and Dad had never taxed any of my allowances or profit shares or other family ventures. Seeing so much money go to taxes was a new kind of sadness in my money-management learning process.

Even after I earned raises at work, and grew old enough to work as much as 15 hours a week, I was still in denial about how much money I was earning because I earmarked over 80% of my money before I even earned it. After paying taxes, I would sock away most of my paychecks in my Roth IRA, which had an annual contribution limit of about $5,000 at the time. The $500 or so I had leftover *in a year* was enough to enjoy a couple of luxuries (like a prepaid cell phone), but was not enough for me to feel like a rich teenager.

If anything, my after-school job taught me that I definitely *needed* to go to college. Sure, I could keep my wage-earning job and make ends meet. But that part-time wage-earning job didn't pay rent, or put a lot of gas in my car (once I was old enough to drive), or buy me much food, or pay for my clothes or cosmetics. In fact, the only reason I could max out my Roth IRA was because I wasn't paying rent, I minimized the amount of driving I did, I had a clothing and cosmetic budget, and I ate from the family fridge.

Basically, having an after-school job taught me how poor I was as a part-time wage earner, and how much richer I could potentially be if I graduated from college with a degree and a real salaried job.

Forget *getting a JOB, Mon*. I needed to *graduate from college, Mon!*

DOUG
More Money, More Problems

When Carol deposited her first check from her Kumon job, she immediately bought herself a pay-as-you-go cell phone.

It wasn't the indulgence that Marge and I thought it might be. We parents had made a classic tech mistake by underestimating the value of this choice. That phone turned out to be a very smart move, and Carol's example taught us how important this connectivity is to a student.

Back in 2006, nearly a year before the first iPhone was announced, we regarded cell phones as a corporate tool. We parents were financially independent and really retired, so we saw no need to spend the money or complicate our lives. We'd finally freed ourselves of having to answer company phone calls from our bosses. We're not Luddites or curmudgeons (not yet, anyway) but we still had a landline and there was no reason to change!

Cell phones were common among college students and teens, not just working adults, but we parents didn't see the need for our daughter to have one.

We declined to buy our daughter a cell phone, yet suddenly our landline phone was driving us nuts. Carol's classmates knew our phone number and assumed that (like everyone else in their group) it was her cell phone. They were frustrated that the number wouldn't receive a text, so they'd call. When they got voicemail (or even worse, a parent), they'd immediately hang up and call back. We had plenty of voice mails that included the phrase,"Urgh, pick up, Carol!" This would happen at all hours of the day and night, to the point where we shut off the ringers and just checked voicemail every day.

Yeah, I know. Clueless parents.

Even worse, we were depriving her of an educational tool and an important school supply item—right up there with calculators and textbooks. Sure, those classmates were calling to gossip. However, they were also forming study groups and working on school projects, and everything was being coordinated via their cell phones. Teen plans for teacher meetings and homework groups were changing by the minute, but nobody worried because they could all text each other the latest update... except for our daughter. She was still living in the 20th century with landlines and e-mail. If she was lucky, the next day at school someone would tell her what she'd missed.

She gave up on educating her parents and simply bought her own phone. The fees were a big expense on a 14-year-old's budget, and back then she had to pay for every text. However she was also back in the loop on school and extracurricular activities.

Our landline stopped ringing.

We parents missed an entire revolution in educational technology. We'd assumed it was a teen toy (or a vanity accessory) like a video game or an iPod. Instead, it was keeping her just as connected as a corporate executive and it helped her react to a rapidly-changing business day. There was still plenty of teen drama (and poor cell phone etiquette) but we all learned to live with it. The payoff was well worth the price.

In retrospect we realized that socializing didn't move online until the early to mid-teen years. At ages 10 or 12 the kids wanted to hang out together in person. They went to each other's houses or to the playground. (Perhaps cell phones were too expensive in the 1990s and early 2000s.) By the time Carol was 14, the district high school had spread their local neighborhood group across town, and a cell phone helped coordinate meetings and projects.

A few months later, Marge bought her own cell phone to help with a volunteer conference. People were carpooling to the presentations and arranging other offsite meetups, and as their plans changed then they'd text everyone... except my spouse.

Suddenly we parents knew (again) how it felt to be left out of the loop when you were trying to do your job.

In a neat, and probably common, case of karmic payback, our daughter showed us how to set up Mom's first cell phone.

Today we recommend adding a cell phone into a family plan at age 12 or 13. (Marge and I can't wait to see how Carol and her spouse handle this rite of passage with their family!) There will be school rules about how your child could use it, of course, and you would also have your limits. You'd also have many conversations about what's appropriate to put online, and today's culture already has plenty of videos (and bad examples) to help with that.

CAROL
Controlling The Chatter, Avoiding the Illegal

Having my own cell phone taught me a lot about staying in control of my social interactions. It was a very basic "brick" phone with a keypad and a screen that only supported texting and calling. So, I only used my phone to call and text with people I wanted to interact with: my friends, class-project teammates, and parents. My phone was also my opportunity to set my own expectations amongst my friends. If my friends sent me a useless "chain text" that I had to pay a quarter to read, I would express my unhappiness with my friends. I turned off my phone after 8 p.m. and during school hours, and made this fact known to my friends.

Teens today are exposed to cyber bullying, unsolicited contact or images, blackmail, (attempted) contraband sales, and even implication for being in group texts involving any of the above activities. I could barely afford to text and call my friends for study groups and weekends out, so I blocked any unknown contacts and didn't pick up calls I didn't recognize. My friends didn't wrangle me into group texts unless it was for a meet up. My parents knew my cell phone number, but my distant relatives did not; I still used the family landline to call relatives.

Mom and Dad respected my limited cell phone use, and only called me when necessary. To encourage me to call whenever I desired, my parents reimbursed me for any phone calls I had with them, whether it was me or my parents who initiated the call.

With today's family cell plans and the multitude of smartphones, consider more creative ways to encourage your kids to save and profit-share when it comes to cell phones. What about an incentive for getting the "bare bones" generic smart phone instead of an expensive iPhone or Samsung smartphone? What about encouraging your kids to use less cell data and more Wi-Fi connectivity, or more messaging apps and less texting? How about downloading survey apps that give your kids gift cards, coupons, or other small incentives for taking surveys or testing out certain products? Because kids are often more tech-savvy than adults, let your kids offer up ideas for profit-sharing and other incentives. They may just figure out novel ways for the whole family to save money!

DOUG
Starting A Roth IRA

Along with our daughter's first job (and her first cell phone) came her first Roth IRA contribution.

This was a big deal to us parents, and we might have been a bit intense when we described its advantages to her. In the 1980s we were a little slow to catch on to our own IRAs, and by 2006 we greatly appreciated how those accounts had grown.

We used all of the classic contribution spreadsheets to demonstrate how an early start would give her IRA more time to grow. We explained all of the tax advantages and showed her how she could invest in stock funds. For a teen, this was serious adulting. It was way better than having your own checkbook in elementary school.

IRAs are another chance to discuss deferred gratification. By this point we parents had been retired for over four years, and our daughter keenly appreciated the benefits of our financial independence. We talked about how she was saving for her own FI (just like her parents) and that Roth IRAs gave her choices.

We described how she could withdraw her contributions at any time with no penalties or taxes. When she was helping us with home improvement projects, we mentioned how she could withdraw a little money from her Roth IRA to buy her first home. We emphasized the penalties that could be charged for other withdrawals, and explained they were an incentive to make sure she saved for financial independence.

She also started hearing from us that a high savings rate could accelerate her journey to FI, and she'd still be able to lead a fun life without feeling deprivation.

Once she understood the basics of the account, we started the discussion about asset allocation.

We tried to keep it simple. She could control how much she saved, what she invested in, and how much its expense ratio cost her. Everything else was beyond an investor's control.

We explained that the volatility of the stock market would randomly put shares on sale, but she would only lose money if she decided to sell her shares. Bear markets and recessions were even bigger sales. We borrowed heavily from Warren Buffett: "When the price of hamburgers goes down, the Buffett household cheers!" Since she was investing her Roth IRA contributions for at least 10 years, she could afford to be aggressive with passive stock index funds using low expense ratios. Her IRA value would be volatile, but she'd regularly buy more shares with every paycheck.

Her challenge was getting comfortable with her asset allocation and not worrying about the markets. She should stay away from the news media and the 24/7 news cycle to focus on the long term. Read websites, and books, and watch videos, but don't worry about the economy or politics. Every investor is different, and she turned out to be on the "index fund investor" end of the bell curve instead of on the "big swingin' day-trader" end.

Those teen financial milestones also led to her first income-tax return. The tax software made it easy for her, and getting back her withholding delivered immediate gratification.

That first job (and her Roth IRA) led to many discussions about good financial behavior. Years later, when she was in college, she showed her classmates how to open their own Roth IRAs.

CAROL
Kid 401(k) to a Roth IRA

I found a Roth IRA more exciting than a Kid 401(k) because the Roth IRA was *real*. Not only did I see the money being deposited in my IRA, but I also received tax paperwork, statements, and other official paperwork indicating that I was a real investor. This wasn't something that Mom and Dad made (or made up) to supplement the lack of legal money-saving vehicles available to minors.

I also learned pretty quickly that I preferred putting my Roth IRA on "auto-pilot." I didn't enjoy having to log in to make a contribution every paycheck; instead, I enjoyed watching the automatic payment go from my checking account to my Roth IRA. I didn't enjoy having to research and re-evaluate hundreds of stock options I could use; instead, I enjoyed picking a mutual fund and letting the dividends automatically reinvest in the fund.

The last big realization was that I didn't want to withdraw funds from my Roth IRA. Maybe this was a good habit leftover from my "untouchable" and "often forgotten about" Kid 401(k). Maybe it was just a "Jedi mind trick" I played on myself so that I enjoyed seeing the numbers "jump higher and higher" when I did remember to log in once every few months. And maybe it was just a reflection of how my parents raised me—never had I ever heard of them withdrawing IRA funds, and I couldn't think of a reason why I should, either.

/////// SUMMARY
Teens Face External Influences, Make Increasingly Complex Choices, and Encounter Changing Technologies

Each family has to make their own choices, and kids mature at different ages. Carol was very responsible with a cell phone at age 14 (as far as we parents knew!). Her credit card at age 13 worked out well, but at age 9 she struggled a little with keeping control of an ATM card.

The teen years are the most common time for kids to start working for money (entry-level jobs), and thus learn more about work and taxes, and even open a Roth IRA.

If your kid is showing financial maturity, consider bigger responsibilities like managing a six-month stretch of allowance, managing their "clothing and cosmetics" budget, and/or new kinds of profit sharing. They may make mistakes (like Carol did), and they may impress you with their ever-growing money management skills (like Carol also did).

Astute readers may have noticed that we didn't use debit cards. That's because we parents were doing fine with ATMs, credit cards, and rewards points. We still don't use debit cards because we just haven't needed them. Today, our choice would be the FamZoo system where parents can set up their kids' debit cards and control their spending limits.

Keep an eye out for board games (and websites, and YouTube channels) to help your teens learn about earning, saving, and spending. Some schools use financial-literacy tools like Cash Flow Crunch to start conversations about wages and life, and those games can help you find more teachable moments with your family.

As parents, you'll see new tech and try to figure out how to use it safely. If you don't, your teens surely will. Keep the lines of communication open and talk about how you'd adapt to having it in your lives.

CHAPTER GOALS

- Ask "What could I do to afford that?" instead of stating "We can't afford that."
- Open a credit card account (authorized user) with a low spending limit.
- Discuss part-time jobs, wages, and income taxes.
- Open a Roth IRA.

CHAPTER SEVEN

Cashing In the Kid 401(k)... and the First Car

> "

> **USED-CAR SELLER:** "DID YOU MANAGE TO FIND A BANK THAT WOULD GIVE YOU CASH?"
>
> **CAROL:** (HOLDING UP A THICK ENVELOPE) "RIGHT HERE!"
>
> **SELLER:** "YOU GOT THE CASH?!?"
>
> USED-CAR SELLER REACTING TO CAROL'S CASH OFFER

DOUG
What Happened With The Kid 401(k)

Like most teens, Carol was very interested in driving. We might have practiced in an empty parking lot for a few months before she got her learner's permit, and after that she piled on the practice hours. She wanted to complete her driver-education requirements and take her road test right after her 16th birthday. She was wrestling our 1994 Ford Taurus station wagon, which was nearly as rugged as an armored truck, but very uncool. To a nervous parent, that car had everything a teen needed for a safe driving experience.

We parents supported her interest in getting her license! We drive far less in Hawaii than we've ever driven on the Mainland, and our rush-hour road skills were rusty. We knew that she needed plenty of local driving experience before she left our nest to live anywhere else.

Frankly we were also happy to have more help with car maintenance and errands. She was already proficient at changing the oil and maintaining tire pressure, and we knew she'd enjoy taking over the family grocery shopping.

As our daughter's 16th birthday approached, we thought she'd be eager to spend her Kid 401(k). We could show her how to find good used cars online, inspect them, test-drive them, and negotiate the price. If she wasn't ready to buy a car yet, she knew she could roll her $5,000 Kid 401(k) balance over to her Bank of Carol CDs. They no longer paid 12% APY (because now she understood percentage math and interest rates) but the Bank of Carol still paid a little more than the local credit union.

We were ready to start the used-car search when she threw us a curveball: she wanted to syndicate her Kid 401(k) money with us for a share of a Toyota Prius hybrid. She'd take care of the car for a couple of years, and she'd do most of the driving. She proposed that when she left home for college, we could then buy her shares back for the same $5,000.

As I remember this conversation, I admit that we parents were eagerly suckered into agreeing with her. I'm a life-long engineering nerd, and Carol has the same interests. We'd read about Priuses and I'd ridden in a couple of them. I was fascinated by hybrid tech and I expected that we'd buy one "someday"—after our current used cars had been driven into the ground, of course.

We parents didn't *need* to buy a hybrid yet, but we wanted to support our daughter's financial initiative (and that Taurus was on its third water pump...). She had proposed the idea without hearing it from us, and she was willing to give up two years of interest in her CDs for our majority ownership of the car. We pointed out that her idea resembled a vehicle lease, and those leases have penalties for excessive wear and tear. If she damaged or neglected the car then there might be deductions against her $5,000 share.

A few weeks later we were the happy family owners of a used 2006 Prius. It had very low mileage and was in great shape so we paid the full used-car value in cash. (It was our only used car which still had a year left on the Toyota warranty!) Our daughter pointed out that it had nearly triple the gas mileage of the 14-year-old Taurus, and the Prius was much easier to drive. Our collision risks were lower, and our operating expenses were much less.

We were pleased with our daughter's ingenuity, and we parents hardly drove that car for the next two years. She took care of her investment with the pride of ownership, and she only lost $200 of her share for a parking-lot dent on the rear bumper. The ding wasn't her fault, but she gained a new defensive awareness of the careless drivers around her.

Better still, we parents drove that Prius for another decade after she left the nest.

CAROL
The Original Surfmobile

Even though I grew up on Oahu, Dad and I didn't learn how to surf until after Dad retired from the Navy. The logic at the time was simple: Dad had co-workers who'd call in sick when the surf was really good, and Dad wanted no distractions at his already high-stress job. After dealing with this for over a decade of Hawaii living, Dad had to find out more about "this whole surfing addiction" once he retired.

And sure enough, Dad and I took our first surfing lesson the weekend after Dad retired. By the end of that lesson, we were both hooked. Many weekends between fifth grade and my first weekend at college were spent driving to the beach to surf.

Arguably, driving was really the only way to go surfing. Sure, I could strap a nine-foot-long surfboard to a bicycle, but that was almost a

25-mile ride one way, and the roads were always unpaved near the beach. I could try to take a surfboard on a city bus, but the city buses at the time weren't designed for carrying surfboards[6]. I couldn't afford a $60 cab ride one way, Uber/Lyft didn't exist yet, and no one else in the neighborhood surfed; everyone else worked such long hours that weekends were for errands, not for surfing.

There was one last thing that cemented my desire to get a driver's license ASAP. In middle school, my bus stop happened to be along the main road that connected my neighborhood to the highway. That meant that most mornings, as I was standing at the bus stop with my friends waiting to go to school, Dad would drive by in the family Taurus with surfboards strapped to the roof, merrily honking his horn and waving at me and my friends. It didn't help that there was a stop sign right at my bus stop, so my friends and I got to spend a full 10 seconds drinking in the scene of my FI surfer dad heading to the beautiful beach instead of commuting like the rest of us.

These mornings may have also cemented my desire to be financially independent myself. I knew that if I wanted to go surfing every morning like Dad did, and not just on the weekends, I had to save a lot of money. If I wanted to save a lot of money, I had to have a good job AND be financially fit. If I wanted to have a good job then I had to get good grades in school. And if I wanted to be financially fit, I had to learn how to take care of my money.

It's funny how Dad's surfing drive-bys became a big motivator in my own FI goals.

---

[6] The State of Hawaii is building its first elevated rail system on Oahu. From the earliest design sketches, they ensured the passenger compartments had room for surfboard storage during transit. The rail has yet to be finished, so I haven't tried this commuting method yet.

DOUG
A Note About Insuring Teen Drivers

We're not insurance experts. Many states (and insurers) charge a hefty premium to insure your teen driver, and it seems far more expensive than it's worth. Maybe you're not even sure that your teen is ready to drive.

Your teen might not even see the need to have a driver's license. On Money Magazine's website, research from the University of Michigan and the Federal Highway Administration shows Millennials and Gen Z with sharply lower rates of licenses among teens.[7] It could be due to smartphones and social media as well as more public transportation options and environmental concerns. If your teen isn't interested in getting behind a wheel then you might decide not to push them.

We parents felt that learning to manage a vehicle was just as important as learning to manage money, and it was best to make all of those mistakes at home. We could afford it because we made it one of our parenting priorities.

Even when your insurer (and your state laws) make it expensive to insure a teen, we feel that their highway driving experience is still worth far more than ignorance.

Our frugal parental driving habits really paid off when we added our daughter to our policy. Here are some financial considerations for your household:

---

[7] "Why There's Been a Huge Decline in Drivers' Licenses for Millennials and Gen X" by Denver Nicks. Money Magazine, January 19, 2016, www.money.com/money/4185441/millennials-drivers-licenses-gen-x/.

- Use an older vehicle.

- Cancel the collision and comprehensive insurance on your teen's vehicle if it is already older and has lost most of its value.

- Many insurers do not charge a premium for a teen with a learner's permit.

- Many insurers offer good-student discounts.

- Many insurers offer a discount for taking a licensed driver's education course.

- Don't buy them a car. If you have more drivers than vehicles on your insurance policy then your teen could get an "occasional driver" discount.

- Your insurer might offer a discount for teen telematics. These devices monitor the driver's behavior and offer audio feedback for excessive acceleration or braking.

Canceling collision and comprehensive insurance is a contentious (and expensive!) gap of coverage. Our family has bought used vehicles since the 1980s and we canceled those insurance options long ago. (The savings went into our fund for the next used car.) New teen drivers can also find perfectly safe used vehicles at a low price. They'll still have the required liability coverage if they get hit by someone else's car. But if they damage their own car, they'll have to pay for their own repairs.

Families with new cars (or luxury models) should certainly consider keeping collision and comprehensive insurance (perhaps with a high deductible). You can decide whether your teen needs to drive those hot cars.

CAROL
How Much Is A New Car Really Worth To You?

Around the same time that I turned 16, I noticed that other classmates who were gifted cars on their Sweet 16th birthday weren't as careful with their cars. Often these classmates would get into avoidable and memorable accidents, like the kid who rear-ended the high school football coach's van. (The coach caught the kid as he attempted to run away on foot from the accident, and the kid was shaking by the time the coach was done yelling at him.) Another classmate of mine totaled three "new" sports cars in a two-year period due to texting and driving. A third classmate was grounded for a whole semester after she "borrowed" her mom's new car without permission, and totaled it that evening a quarter mile from her home on a notoriously tight street corner that also happened to be a school bus stop. And in all cases, it was a good reminder that my peers could easily do the same damage to "MY" car too, if they were to hit me in an accident or even got behind the wheel of my car.

Watching my peers got me thinking: why would I buy a brand-new car if one of my careless peers could total it whenever and wherever? What if it got smashed in a parking lot while I was inside a nearby store? What if it got stolen and was never found again? Why would I spend so much money on one thing if that one thing could be here today and gone tomorrow? And to lose so much money in one accident...I shuddered at the idea.

Speaking of return on investment, about once a year, Mom and Dad would have me enter the family Prius's information on the Kelley Blue Book website (kbb.com), and check to see how much the car was worth year after year. Watching the Prius' value plummet from $21,000 to $16,000 over a two year period was incredible—that was all of my "syndicated investment" gone in a fraction of the eight years it took to earn it! It was another great reminder as to why I should take care of cars, and think twice about buying a brand-new car when I could have two or three or even four (!) used cars for the same price.

DOUG
Running The Household Errands

Once our daughter was street-legal, we parents offloaded all the errands and chores that we could think of.

As a minority owner of the Prius, our daughter was responsible for filling it with gas. (We reimbursed her for miles spent on errands because we felt that it was important to gain the driving experience.) She took care of the oil changes and other fluids. She had to wash it for free, but she could still earn money by washing our other car.

The biggest chore was grocery shopping. (This was especially helpful because teens eat more calories than parents!) We all kept up with the household grocery list, and she earned her usual half of the coupon savings. We even motivated her by paying a 5% delivery fee, which usually worked out to $5-$6 a trip. She charged the groceries to her credit card and kept the rewards points.

We parents also thought that she'd enjoy the grocery adulting experience. She was in charge of finding everything on the list and buying it in the most cost-efficient quantities. She could take as much time as she wanted to explore the aisles and try new products. She was testing out new recipes, and she had to figure out the ingredients. She learned the prices of everything and could start judging their value. She had to talk with the cashiers and keep an eye on the transaction.

I didn't set foot in a grocery store for nearly two years.

We parents thought it was important for a teen to learn all they could about running a food budget. She seemed to make a good impression at the grocery store, too. It's been over five years since her last grocery run yet some of the employees still ask us how our daughter is doing.

CAROL
Buying And Raising Cars

While the Prius was my first co-owned car, I still miss my first solo-owned car, Ekahi, or 'Eka (the Hawaiian word for "One"). That sweet old car was a 1999 Honda CR-V that had 163,000 miles and 13 years on her when I purchased her back in 2012 in Houston, TX. By the time I traded her in for my second car (named...'Elua, the Hawaiian word for "Two"), I traded in 'Eka for $1,500 off the price of 'Elua. At that point, 'Eka had nearly 200,000 miles and 18 years on her, and had been all the way to Spain and back, literally.

Deciding to buy the CR-V actually started with some other skills learned in my Freshman year of college. My college campus participated in a program called Zipcar, which allows account holders (like me) to rent cars for hours at a time (the rate was $8 an hour when I was in college). My friends and I loved Zipcars because we could get to our favorite mall for a fraction of the cost of a local taxi. This was also in the years before Uber and Lyft really took off.

The cars offered by Zipcar changed routinely, so I got to "test drive" a bunch of models, like Honda CR-Vs, Ford Fiestas, Toyota Camrys, and so on. When it came to buying my first car that I would own completely, I simply bought a month's subscription to ConsumerReports.com, and searched all of my favorite models from

Zipcar. It turns out that older CR-V models had more reliable engines than Ford Fiestas, they could fit a bike in the cargo space, and they were cheaper.

The day I bought my car was a long day with a great reward. Dad and I met with the seller I found on Craigslist, and we test-drove the car on the local Houston highways. We also swung by a local mechanic who, for a $100 fee, gave me an accurate appraisal of the car's maintenance and any upcoming maintenance issues I might encounter. The $100 was well worth it—the mechanic pointed out $500 in maintenance costs I would need in the next month, and I convinced the seller that I'd buy his car for $500 less than he offered, but all in cash that I literally had in hand for him.

After his eyes bugged out at the stuffed envelope of cash, he accepted the deal on the spot.

Two years after I bought the CR-V, I landed a chance-of-a-lifetime assignment with the Navy in Rota, Spain. The Navy will ship one car for free overseas, so my car got a free ride to Spain. She was a little beat up from all her years stateside, and fit in perfectly with all the other "Rota beaters" frequenting the narrow cobblestone roads, hard turns, and other crazy aspects of Spanish roads. She was a great adult starter car and adventure car.

By the time I'd had 'Eka for four years, she'd taught me a lot about car repair. Once, I accidentally broke off an interior door handle while moving a friend's apartment furniture, and I learned how to look up the part, order it on Amazon, and install the new handle with some assistance from YouTube. The same thing happened a few years later, when a small plastic part connected to the brake signal broke off, keeping the brake lights perpetually on as I drove. I again found the replacement part and consulted YouTube for a quick repair. But after the starter motor failed on a busy July 4th weekend (ironically in the parking lot of the local auto parts store), I got a pay raise at work, and my new assignment stateside had me working upwards of 80 hours a week (!), I needed a better car without unexpected repairs.

Buying 'Elua was pretty similar to buying 'Eka. I started with a one-month subscription to ConsumerReports.com, and decided this time I wanted a Toyota RAV-4. Because I had very little free time, I opted for a convenient used car dealership instead of the time-consuming Craigslist ads. After trading in 'Eka for $1,500 and re-negotiating the final price tag for paying in "cash" (really a paper check that the dealership would deposit the same day I wrote it), I got my new 2011 RAV-4 for a cool $11,000 in 2016.

Fast forward to the present, where my husband and I recently went down to a one-car lifestyle. I'd left Active Duty for the Reserves, which meant I was working part-time. He is a military student spending the majority of his day on campus, so a bicycle was handier than a car. We live in base housing close to his school, so he bicycles to and from class with his uniform carefully stowed in a "garment pannier," a saddlebag that easily fits on his bicycle. The one car we own spends four of seven days a week sitting in the garage. We use it for hauling groceries, appointments out in town too far to walk or bike to, driving to and from church, and of course, for surfing!

My husband K.J. and I decided that if we were going to have one car, we would get a very fuel-efficient car that would save gas money in the long run, and was a "kid friendly" car for the family we were planning to start. So I sold my 8-year-old RAV-4 to K.J.'s younger brother, and K.J. traded in his 2012 Volkswagen Jetta (worth about $3,300 in 2019), to get a discount off our "new" 2015 Prius V. When we bought the Prius V in 2019, we paid the $19,000 price via check; once again, we raised eyebrows at the dealership and were told "we don't get cash very often...give us a moment while we review our policy on accepting checks."

So in the 10 years I've been driving, I've moved six times, lived in two countries, and in five different states, I've never had to buy a new car, I've never had to pay a car loan, and I've never been "stranded" by my used cars. I've learned a lot of life skills and increased my self-confidence.

SUMMARY
The Kid 401(k) Was A Huge Motivator For Our Teen To Be A Long-term Saver And Investor.

The Kid 401(k) started with a birthday celebration and a big jump in allowance—and it also offered the "free money" of parental matching contributions. The table in Appendix A can help you build your own and show your child how much it'll grow each year.

We were surprised and impressed with our teen's initiative of using her 401(k) for a share of our Prius, and it saved our family hundreds of dollars for teen-driver insurance. Her financial incentives for household errands and grocery shopping gave her more driving experience. It also helped her develop her adulting skills while she was still at home to talk about them with her parents.

CHAPTER GOALS

- Celebrate reaching a savings goal: the maturing of the Kid 401(k)!
- Challenge your teen to find affordable driving insurance (and to qualify for discounts).
- Offer privileges and commissions for accident-free driving and running errands.

CHAPTER EIGHT

Adulting

You're trying to reconcile the beautiful home that your mother kept that you lived in growing up, with the beautiful home that, like, Pinterest says you're supposed to have. And the fact that you have no...money, so...

ILIZA SCHLESINGER
ELDER MILLENNIAL COMEDY SHOW

DOUG
Manage Your Teen's Expectations About The Education Fund

I'll repeat an opinion from Chapter 1: the size of the education fund is your personal choice, and it depends on your values as well as your savings rate.

Whatever you decide is the appropriate amount for an education fund, you should start managing your teen's expectations in middle school. Their teachers are already piling on the expectations, and they might be stressing your kid with their pressure.

All of these discussions about life after high school might improve the way your teen behaves during high school. By reviewing the finances of post-high school education before high school starts, your teen may find their own motivation for excelling at school.

One approach could be to tell your kids that you're willing to pay for two years at a community college, or a certain number of semesters at a state university. The rest is their challenge. Talk with them about work-study programs, scholarships, and even student loans.

Back in 1992, while Marge and I were still on active duty with steady paychecks, we decided to contribute enough each month to the college fund to pay for at least four years at a state university. We wanted to give the fund as much compounding time as possible before we left active duty for other careers.

At first we invested our contributions very aggressively in an equity index fund (100% stocks). As the contributions and the funds compounded over the years, we realized that the fund could grow big enough to pay for most private universities. Marge and I were earning more in our careers and our high savings rate was on track for our financial independence, so we kept up our contributions. Whatever Carol didn't use could continue to grow for graduate degrees or other certifications.

When Carol turned 13 years old, we stopped buying stock funds and started buying bonds. When she turned 15 we began cashing out a portion of the stock fund each for a ladder of three-year CDs. By the time she graduated from high school, her college fund was mostly CDs and bonds. During her college freshman year we cashed out the last of the equity fund and bought the final three-year CD.

The sooner your teens understand what the family's finances will cover, the better they can figure out how they want to handle their education. Maybe they aren't even interested in college in the first place, and they'll have enough funds for a trade school leading to a professional license. Good electricians can earn even more than good plumbers, and neither one of those careers can be outsourced overseas.

CAROL
Start Talking About Post-High School In Middle School

Plan more specific details for "life after high school" as early as middle school, such as what classes or interests kids want to pursue in the ramp-up to high school graduation. My parents started the discussion at the end of my seventh grade year, when I was selecting eighth grade electives. I could take "fun" electives like learning how to play an 'ukulele (a standard option in Hawaii), or I could opt for more academic electives, like algebra. I was also pressured by my middle school into taking after-school academics, like the traveling school orchestra and competitive band. This turned into a healthy and positive debate in the Nordman household.

After weighing the pros and cons, I decided to go for the academic electives because I would get the subject practice early. If I didn't do well in algebra in middle school, I could take it again in high school, where I would have a "second chance." But doing well in middle school algebra actually had a bigger advantage than "trying something harder out." Taking advanced academic classes in middle school led to "validations" and "boosts" in high school math courses, and even time to take AP or IB courses instead of the "regular" equivalents. Those academic courses could lead to collegiate-level math classes (at a local community college) while I was still finishing up high school. In theory, I could then take the transfer credit from that community college math course to the local four-year university, which meant I didn't have to take basic math courses again. I could graduate college earlier, or add more classes towards a masters degree while still working towards my undergraduate degree. In the long run, I spent less time repeating material while simultaneously saving tuition money.

Oh, and if I didn't take those traveling and competitive after-school academics, then the money NOT spent on travel would compound interest in the education fund instead.

I'd known since about the age of 8 that Mom and Dad were saving enough money for me to go to college; this was a casual statement in one of many family meetings, but it stuck with me. I also knew that it was solely up to me to study, get good grades, get into college, and graduate. I personally never considered an alternative to college; I wanted a college degree.

It wasn't until my teen years and a fateful trip to visit a Navy friend of Mom and Dad's that I started considering joining the military after college, and specifically the Navy because I loved water and wanted to "see the world." I spent most of high school debating the many ways to join the Navy before I decided that a Navy Reserve Officers' Training Corps (ROTC) scholarship suited me best. With an ROTC scholarship, my tuition and books would be paid for, I'd get a free set of uniforms (worth thousands of dollars, surprisingly), and I'd participate in a schedule of military-related training, including near-daily physical training and weekly military classes and events. By the time I graduated college I'd earn a commission as an officer in the U.S. Navy. After graduation, I would owe the Navy eight years of service. I saw the ROTC scholarship as a fantastic way to go to college for nearly free and have a guaranteed job after graduation, with more day-to-day collegiate freedom than a military academy offers.

All that being said, my ROTC scholarship didn't cover everything. Mom and Dad's education fund paid for my room and board and plane tickets to school and home on breaks. There were times that I considered using education fund money for things like spring break trips or special events. But then I'd remember (or be reminded by Mom and Dad) that I'd miss out on the compounding interest and profit sharing benefits later if I spent college fund money now.

As promised, when I graduated from college, Mom and Dad paid out my half of the profit-sharing of the education fund through annual tax-free gifts (discussed in Chapter 10). Technically, I could've left the money in the education fund and earmarked it for graduate degrees. But at the time I wasn't interested in earning a graduate degree. As of this writing, I'm still not interested in earning a graduate degree.

DOUG
Manage Expectations After High School And Offer Financial Incentives

When you've aligned your teen's motives with your financial incentives (see Chapter 5), then you can extend this technique to life after high school.

Explain that when young adults leave home, they'll reset their standards and have to live frugally. They're starting out with a lot less money and lifestyle, just like when Mom and Dad were starting their careers all those years ago. (They've seen your pictures, right?) Your kids are not going to have the same quality of shelter (let alone entertainment) as they did while growing up in your house!

Ideally, they'd achieve the minimum living standards in a safe neighborhood with roommates and affordable public transportation (or a reliable vehicle). At the same time, when they learn to live frugally they can build a cash cushion as a solid defense against unpleasant surprises like emergency car repairs or even layoffs.

Next, you parents aren't obligated to pay for their college degree or a trade certification. You can negotiate a compromise like work-study, or suggest that you'll pay for two years at a community college. Remind them that student loans are a two-edged sword which can boost their income with a lucrative skill, or cripple them with five figures of debt.

Whether or not they want to go to college, let them know that any scholarships they earn are theirs to keep. (We parents were greatly surprised to learn how many alumni scholarships went begging for applications—every semester!) Students can use scholarship-search apps and visit colleges' offices of alumni relations and financial aid to research more opportunities.

Review the costs of tuition and potential negligence: "Missing an 8:00 am class wastes $102.31 of your college fund and could delay your graduation by another semester." Let them spend the money for their room and board, whether they hand it over to the college dorm (and eat in the cafeteria) or live off-campus (and cook for themselves). If they choose to live off-campus (with roommates) instead of in the dorm (with roommates!), then they get to keep whatever cash is left over at the end of the semester.

Regardless of their majors, encourage your young adults to take business classes. These are helpful not just for accountants and entrepreneurs but also for engineers, scientists, doctors, and lawyers—and most especially for liberal-arts majors. They'll learn what the business majors (and marketers) are going to do to them unless they learn the techniques for their own self-defense. They might also learn that they want to run their own business.

Here's a bold idea: consider handing over a semester of college money to your young adult. Let them manage their own education. You've worked for this moment for over a decade. Now you'll really find out if they're ready to take care of larger sums of money!

You can even offer a new financial incentive: when your student is a good steward of the education fund, then there will be profit-sharing after college. Leave it at that and let them figure out the rest.

CAROL
Celebrations And Rites Of Passage

If your family has a different perspective on funding your teen's post-high school education, your family may also look at some celebrations and rites of passage differently. For us Nordmans, we realized that we highly valued earning a high school diploma, and attending college, but the high school graduation ceremony itself was not valuable to us.

Here's how my high school ran graduation the year I graduated. All graduating seniors had to pay around $75 to buy brand-new—not rent or borrow or buy used—single-use mustard-gold graduation robes and shiny brown stoles. Seniors were also given a strict dress code for what to wear under the gown; for girls, it had to be a white dress, at least touching the knees, with shoulder straps no less than one inch wide, and white shoes or sandals with one to three inches in the heel. Girls were not allowed to wear pants and a collared shirt with a neutral tie like the boys were allowed to.

My graduating class of over five hundred students was so big that we couldn't hold graduation anywhere on the high school campus grounds, even in the football stadium. Instead, graduation would be a 45-minute drive to the college football stadium downtown. All Seniors were required to report to school on two Saturday mornings prior to graduation day to practice loading the graduation school buses, and then do a dress rehearsal in the college football stadium. Each practice event was at least four hours long, and the tropical weather was hot enough that each Senior was "issued" bottled water to drink during the practices. This was a costly experience in time and real money.

And that wasn't the only sticker shock experience for graduating Seniors. In the fall semester of Senior Year, we were required to attend a special "ring rally" in the high school gym, where we were given a flashy presentation from the ring company and an order form (in addition to the online store link) to buy our high school rings. I debated spending my own money on my high school ring for days; Mom and Dad quickly pointed out that neither of them got any joy out of their high school rings, but their wedding bands and academy rings meant much more to them. I decided to follow suit, and am still immensely glad I did.[8]

Separately, the parents were bombarded with "packages" and ads to buy all kinds of graduation stuff: senior photoshoot sessions, special invitations for relatives made in parchment paper (including shiny address stickers), glass picture frames to hold the graduation photo, "SEN10R" brand clothes and shirts for my graduating class of 2010, an extra tassel to keep as "graduation memorabilia," and even special frames for the high school diploma, which was just a half sheet of paper. Any family could easily spend over $1,000 on stuff before traveling for graduation events and all the parties kicked off.

And $1,000 is about the price of a brand-new, custom-made surfboard.

It felt like A LOT of time and money to spend on a simple, two-hour-long ceremony. To spend hours shopping for a white dress I'd never

---

[8] Note: my maternal grandparents, whose own parents were U.S. immigrants, highly value a college education, and bought my college ring for me as a graduation gift. It's still one of my most treasured possessions, and I wear it whenever I can. They didn't tell me they would buy my ring until I told them I got the order form in my senior year of college.

find in my size, then having it tailored, searching for shoes that I probably had to buy online and pay trans-Pacific shipping costs for, robes that would only be worn once, and then to take two Saturday mornings off work (which I really enjoyed) to go to a graduation practice just seemed like too much of a time and money investment.

Since the rest of the family couldn't attend graduation (they were too far away and this was before graduations were live-streamed), my parents and I realized that there was no point to me attending the graduation ceremony. We double-checked with the school, and learned there was no requirement to "walk" at my graduation ceremony in order to receive my high school diploma. In fact, Seniors were going to receive a "fake" diploma at the ceremony, and would have to go back to school the following Tuesday to pick up the real diploma.

Instead of spending time and money on my graduation ceremony, my parents and I jointly decided that I wouldn't participate. I still went to (and thoroughly enjoyed) the after party with my friends, paid for by my parents. Instead of splitting the profits for the ceremony, Dad and I pooled the money to buy a brand-new, custom-made surfboard. More than a decade later, my "graduation present" is still used at the Nordman household by whomever is around to enjoy the good surf. In fact, anyone who has had a surfing lesson from my Dad may have learned how to surf on the "graduation present." That was a far more joyful purchase than mustard-yellow robes and an extra tassel. That surfboard has seen thousands of hours of fun, instead of one two-hour ceremony.

For the record, my high school diploma still sits in its original cardboard holster somewhere in my book case. My college diploma is the one proudly hanging up on a wall in our home.

In many ways, this final financial decision was a graduation from the lessons my parents had taught me. I spent my time and energy on what I valued, instead of "following the crowd" and bowing to peer (and even family) pressure.

DOUG
"You're On Your Own!": A Parent's Letters To An 18-Year-Old

As Carol grew up, she began to challenge our authority. We parents saw that behavior as a compliment to our parenting skills, not a confrontation. We were still the grownups, we still had the power, and we were not even really being provoked. We realized that we'd created a safe and loving home where a youngster could act out her "worst" behavior. As a teen, her rebellions helped her flex her fledgling wings of independence and get ready to leave the nest.

Marjorie Savage describes these changes in her book *You're On Your Own (But I'm Here If You Need Me)*. When your teen returns home after an extended absence (a college break, or travel, or the military) it might be similar to hosting a foreign exchange student in your house.

This foreign visitor would be different from you, with different hairstyles and clothing choices, and many other cultural variations. As a host, you'd be fascinated by their background and their lifestyle and by the influences which made them who they are. You'd want to get to know them better.

Then Ms. Savage points out that it's the same with your young adult. If they show up with a spiked mohawk, piercings, tattoos, and Goth fashions... it's not a challenge to your family values or even your parenting. It's probably not about you at all. It's your progeny expressing their adult independence in their own way.

If anything, your parenting has helped them feel comfortable with their new expressions. Relax and get to know this stranger a little better. It could be the beginning of a beautiful new friendship.

While my spouse and I were in college, we spent years stumbling through the minefields of our parents' expectations. I remember being particularly confused by how often my parents expected letters and phone calls, and how I'd spend my breaks. (This was back during the Second Millennium, before the World Wide Web and smartphones, when woolly mammoths roamed the earth.) At age 18 I had a new interpretation of their old rules like "curfew" and "sleepovers."

When our daughter left home for college in 2010, my spouse and I reflected on our college memories. We decided to seize the initiative and set out the ground rules for further discussion. We're not control freaks—we were just trying to do for the next generation what we wish had been done for us. We clarified the confusion with our parents' letter to an 18-year-old.

Until Carol turned 18, her checking account and her credit card were still held jointly with me. (We were both eager to end that part of our relationship!) She also had plenty of other things on her mind during her first semester of college. At the time we wrote this letter (all right, it was an e-mail) she was struggling with homework, exams, ROTC workouts, and her personal spending habits.

Feel free to use this and modify it for your family:

Happy birthday!

Your 18th birthday also marks your independence from the family payroll and the end of our $$$ gifts at birthdays and holidays. You'll still be reimbursed for tuition expenses that ROTC doesn't cover, and our college fund will pay your cell phone bill. Of course both of those subsidies will expire when you graduate!

The last payment to your clothing/cosmetics budget will happen next month. After that... well... you're an engineering major, so nobody will be surprised if you're ragged and stinky. You could always tell people that you're considering joining the submarine force like Dad.

Mom and I aren't sending a consistent message yet, but you should attempt to live your life as if we're not giving you any more money ever. As you build up your personal property (like your collection of military uniforms) then you should consider insuring it so that you won't have to call "Mommy and Daddy" to subsidize a recovery from theft/floods/fires. You already know we're not planning to contribute to your first home, either, because you'll be saving for your own down payment.

Of course we'll buy you the plane tickets

to visit home anytime. When we get together we'll still take you out for meals and pick up the check, but there's a very good chance that in 60 years you'll have to reciprocate our generosity by helping to feed me *my* food.

In the distant future, as the parents of the prospective bride, I think we're paying a chunk of your wedding expenses—a subject to be revisited waaaaay later. We'll also spoil your (maybe someday) kids with a trip to a Disney theme park once or twice a year, and we'll take them off your hands for an occasional sleepover or grandparents weekend. However, we don't want to provide childcare so that you can go to work or stand weekend duty. We want to be "Reserve Grandparents": one weekend a month and two weeks a year. We'd rather not care for the grandkids while you're on deployment, either, but we understand if that's necessary.

During this Christmas break (assuming you want to spend it at home!) we'll spend 20 minutes a day on these financial independence tasks:

- transferring your Roth IRA to your new custodian,

- setting up your CDs at your credit union,

- splitting out your checking account from Dad's account,

- getting your own credit card,

- getting quotes for personal-property insurance, and

- your income-tax returns.

I have a separate lifetime offer for you, not as "Dad" but as "Coach." Mom and I have learned a lot of financial skills over the years (many of them the hard way). We can share the pros and cons of nearly every major financial decision (including marriage and kids). Please feel free to make your own independent decisions without consulting us. But before you sign any paperwork, you could tell whoever's offering you a "good deal" that you want to discuss it with your financial adviser—and then give us a call. We'll show you where to educate yourself, what issues to consider, and what options you might want to choose. We promise not to criticize your lifestyle or your standards, although we may make a lame joke or two about our young-adult years.

We don't intend to hurt your feelings with any of these paragraphs. If we evoked that reaction then please call us and we'll talk about it.

SEND

A few weeks after that letter, our daughter finished her first semester. She said that she was more than ready to come home for the holidays, so we sent her another "what to expect" e-mail:

Since you're returning home in a few weeks, we should warn you about a family-rules change:

There won't be any rules.

We feel that you're coming home as a special houseguest, not just as "our kid." Frankly, your mother and I are more interested in being life coaches and mentors than parents. We'll always be your Mom and Dad, but we think we'll all benefit from a transition to adulthood!

When you get home there won't be any chores or nagging or questions about your homework or where you're going or who you're seeing or any of that other fun stuff from the good ol' days. Sorry.

Just try to be a good houseguest and we'll figure things out as we go. For example, you know that getting off the streets by midnight is still a good safety plan—but Mom and I won't be checking up on you.

SEND

CAROL
Changes And Cutting The Financial Umbilical Cord

When I got the above letter from my parents, it was like they were reading my mind. Already in the one semester I'd been away at college, I was changing. I hadn't undertaken any wardrobe makeovers, but already I was talking and thinking differently than I did in high school. It was a relief to know I was always welcome at home, and this time I would be welcomed as an adult!

Speaking of adulthood, most kids go to college at age 18, when they're legally adults. At the same time they launch from the nest, the consequences are real. Gone are the days where Mom and Dad can bail out my credit card without me paying interest or a penalty. Gone are the days where my credit score won't take a hit.

It's a good thing I learned my credit card lessons while I was still a minor in high school.

I firmly believe that minors should learn about credit by at least having their own credit card *before* they become legal adults. Kids should get a credit card in their teen years, whether independently or linked to their parent's account. I also firmly believe that once a kid turns 18, when they're legally an adult, they should have only their own independent credit card that enables them to "act like an adult." I say all this because that's what my family did, and I still see the benefits today as I live out my twenties. It was especially obvious in college how much more mature I was (money-wise) with my independent credit card and independent income stream, compared to other students that were using parent-linked credit cards and living their college years with *all* expenses paid by their parents.

I didn't (and still don't) agree with the method where parents link their college student's credit card to their account so that they can "watch over them just in case something bad happens" or "get them a better deal because they have no credit history." What I saw happening among my classmates was that family fights would ensue about how the student was spending "the parents' money." Often I would hear stories from my fellow students about daily or weekly calls from parents asking about a recent credit card transaction they "noticed" in their statement or via phone alert. In these phone calls, parents would attempt to, um, "parent" their student over the phone, and the student would receive the "parenting" with an immature attitude. The students were insulted by these calls, and would complain about it to their peers (like me!) instead of having a conversation about it with their parents.

Once again, I deeply appreciated the "privacy" Mom and Dad gave me with my money during my childhood. Even in the earliest days of my childhood when I asked for cash, Mom and Dad never asked "why" or "what for?" Mom and Dad never read a bank statement of mine unless I asked for their help. I never realized that one of the most subtle ways my parents had "treated me like an adult" was by letting me have privacy over how I spent my money, the same way I had privacy in the bathroom or privacy on phone calls made to the house's landline. My parents had only stepped in when I was about to overspend my money, and even then they didn't ask me what I had spent my money on.

The healthiest way I witnessed students going through college was when the family had a clear boundary about who would pay for what during the college years. Many of our parents paid for tuition, books, on-campus meals, and housing that was not already covered by scholarships or work-study programs. I observed that making the student pay for these expensive categories by working long hours was often a recipe for failing out of college altogether. "The line" was often drawn at "fun" money or "spending cash;" parents expected their students to generate their own income for nights off-campus, party supplies, or other fun events.

The students with boundaries often got a job or other income stream of their own to pay for weekends out, flat screen TVs for their dorms, or other purchases parents didn't want to pay for. These jobs would usually be 15 hours or less per week, leaving plenty of time for studying and classes.

There were many ways to earn money on college campuses. For example, as an ROTC scholar, I got a "stipend" of a few hundred dollars, and my particular unit had a "scholarship" from an anonymous donor of a few hundred dollars per semester, depending on the merits of each midshipman. I also worked some weekday and weekend mornings as a campus tour guide. Other friends "manned the front desk" at the gym and various buildings all over campus (a convenient way to study and earn money simultaneously), worked as a Teaching Assistant in their later college years, or joined one of the many tutoring or baby-sitting/nanny firms that LOVED having smart college students in their ranks. The tutoring and baby-sitting firms were the most profitable at $20 per hour, but students had to drive off-campus to make those appointments.

If the student played their cards right, some temporary jobs would also lead to valuable skills needed for their majors, or even a real job in the future. Some students found jobs working at a professor's private consulting firm or assisting in one of the hospitals across the street (my university was adjacent to Houston's Medical District, and a lot of my classmates were pre-med majors). My university also had a great relationship with local alumni, who preferred having summer interns from their alma mater at their booming companies.

Not only did students use these summer paychecks to pay for college expenses, but some of these companies were so thrilled with their student's performance that they welcomed back the former intern for a full-time position once they graduated college. The other students that had to go job hunting were especially envious of these "easy interns."

CAROL
Living Like A Monk

I can still hear Mom laughing as she said, *"Oh girl, you're going to be living like a monk the first year of college!"*

Boy was she right. I was used to the comforts of using Mom and Dad's appliances powered by Mom and Dad's payments to utility companies and all under Mom and Dad's roof. Though I could argue that I helped with maintaining that house, I certainly didn't pay the property taxes or pay for any of the fixtures and the appliances that wore down over the years. I'd gotten comfortable with hardly studying through high school, watching TV every day, and hanging out with friends in my free time. I had a car I could hop in and drive it all around my island home.

Now that I was on my own, I found myself living in a college dorm with just enough clothing and personal possessions to fill two suitcases. Of course, the furniture had been provided by the university and my uniforms had been courtesy of my ROTC scholarship, but everything else I'd either carried in a suitcase or since purchased out of necessity (like bath towels and bed sheets). My new laptop became my personal assistant, and thanks to my course load, I went weeks at a time without watching 'real' TV. My dorm mates became my friends, my bicycle became my primary mode of transportation, and I only left campus maybe once or twice a week.

At the same time, living like a monk made me realize what I truly valued. Suddenly laundry became a valuable errand and not a loathed chore. I didn't feel like clothes shopping because I was happy with the many free, quality t-shirts I was getting at campus events[9] (and like Dad said, no one cares how the engineers dress in class). I so rarely used a TV that I didn't have one again until I was married and living with my husband. Spending $100 on a quality backpack was worth it, considering I took it everywhere with me, and I still have that backpack a decade later. Having an iPad that could take photos of blackboards and quickly back up notes to a cloud was also important for studying and reducing the sheer weight of notebook and textbook paper in my backpack. When it rains (really, it POURS in Houston!) it was also much easier to slip an iPad into a waterproof plastic bag than it was to encase a stack of textbooks and notebooks.

As for entertainment, college students have a wealth of free and reduced-cost entertainment options. My dorm was across the street from a public park with an outdoor auditorium, which regularly hosted free concerts and shows. Downtown Houston (connected by a short and cheap metro ride subsidized by the university) offered professional level theater shows and professional sports games, which the university happily offered subsidized tickets to. I had talented friends majoring in music and theater, and they were always eager to see familiar faces in their audiences. With this wealth of cheap entertainment, I experimented, and quickly learned what I liked and didn't like.

---

[9] Those t-shirts were of such quality that I still have them today—as a t-shirt quilt. There are many companies that will take a stack of old t-shirts and sew a quality blanket out of them for a $100-$200 fee. I used Project Repat, and I sent off my t-shirts right after graduation weekend. I happily received the quilt when I was assigned to my first ship, and it was a comforting piece of "home" to have while underway.

By living like a monk and experimenting with cheap entertainment, I actually got better at budgeting and deciding WHAT I wanted to spend my money on; I learned what brought me joy. Living like a monk meant I spent like a monk, and I started taking better care of my possessions. The best part about college, money-wise, was that I had a fresh start, and I was practicing financial independence while living away from my parents.

Now if only I could have complete financial independence from working...

CAROL
A Note On Textbooks

By my junior year of college, I had mastered spending $100 or less a semester on books across five or more classes, and usually recouped about 70-90% of the money I spent. The secret was in book trades, Amazon.com's used book section, and textbook-savvy websites like Chegg.com. My dorm, as well as my engineering department, both had book trade setups where students could sell and buy the next year's books via publically-available Google Spreadsheets. As I'm writing this book, I'm also learning that there are a lot of online book databases students can also tap; for example, my alma mater now heralds a database called OpenStax, and the company has an app for downloading textbooks to students' devices.

When a paper textbook is still required in class, I also learned that a used book was better than a new book; often the used books had great notes in the margins from previous owners. Sometimes there were witty jokes that broke up the monotony of long study sessions. Other times there would be sections colorfully highlighted with a note saying, "this was covered on the test!"

The other nice thing about used textbooks was all the money I saved in the college fund. By not spending that money on books, I could let those unused dollars grow with compounding interest. I sometimes joked that I saved money on books so that I could afford a life after college.

I do not recommend sharing textbooks amongst friends in the interest of saving money, especially if they live in a different dorm room or have different class schedules. Even if the books are used in "shifts," someone always winds up "hogging" the book, and both parties find themselves stressed out about keeping track of the book. If that book got eaten by an off-campus pet or dropped in a deep rain puddle—game over!

DOUG
Here's What Happens When You Offer Financial Incentives To A Young Adult

Once again our progeny surprised us with her creative life hacks at college. She crowdsourced ideas that we'd never thought of and came up with her own innovations.

The next college issue was moving off-campus. It turned out to be a very good idea.

Our daughter's university was expanding their student population faster than they were building new dorms. When they "volun-told" her to live off-campus during junior and senior years, she was frustrated at figuring out yet another new budget. She didn't know whether she could find an affordable apartment, and living off-campus made it a lot harder to drop by the student cafeteria for meals.

Some of this budget stress boiled over at home during her summer break, and once again we clueless parents were caught by surprise. After a few intense family discussions, we came up with another profit-sharing idea.

Instead of us parents paying the college for yet another semester of room and board, we gave that money to Carol. She could choose her own lifestyle: a nice apartment and frugal food, or a cheap group home with more eating out. Her challenge was making the money last through the holidays for six months (instead of just the semester), but she could keep whatever was left over.

We didn't even have to talk about her choices. She instantly found two roommates (in a two bedroom apartment). She scoured Pinterest for recipes. She shopped for groceries in bulk and used once-a-week kitchen prep to turn raw ingredients into 15-20 healthy meals for the following week. She even put a lock on a closet door and rented it out to dorm friends who needed extra storage.

These weren't just life hacks—they were financial independence boosters. As far as we parents could tell, she didn't expand her lifestyle. Her excess funds went into savings and investments for her life after college.

CAROL
Celebrational Stuff, Part II

Every major milestone in a child's life is an opportunity to make unique financial decisions. One of those milestones is college graduation.

First, let me say that college graduation was a lot more sophisticated than high school graduation, and there was far less to buy. There were no dress code requirements, no pre-event practices, no catalogue of graduation gear, and the graduation robes were (thankfully) the usual black color and could be purchased new or used. Class rings were their own separate ordering and celebration process, held at the beginning of Senior year.

But then, there's really no standard for presents for a recent college grad. Technically, there's no reason to get a college grad a present after the family (may have) just funded the grad's college education. College graduation is another event when money can empower unique financial decisions.

Since I graduated from college and started my new job as a naval officer on the same day, I was already making preparations to move (on the Navy's dime) to my new duty station in Spain. Mom and Dad saw a unique opportunity and graduation gift that I never thought of: they gifted me whatever furniture I wanted from my childhood home. This was a brilliant move by Mom and Dad, yet a move that confused a lot of other money-gifting parents around them on graduation day.

Mom and Dad gifted the old furniture for several reasons:

One, they were offering all of their old, sturdy, dinged-up furniture that had already survived two decades of overseas military moves, and would probably survive (maybe) another couple of military moves before the furniture collapsed from all the trans-oceanic shipping. Mom and Dad were ensuring that I had $0 invested in "my furniture."

Two, because the Navy was moving "my" stuff, Mom and Dad didn't have to pay for removing the old furniture from their house. Instead of budgeting for a "junk removal" or "furniture recycling" service, Mom and Dad could use that money on new furniture. It was a great way to get rid of "old" furniture at zero expense.

Three, I didn't have to figure out how to furnish a place in a foreign country whose language I barely spoke, and with a job that left me with little free time. I could focus on my job instead of on my living arrangements.

Four, Mom and Dad had already put in a three-month "reservation" to visit my place in Spain, which would save them a lot of money when they visited Euro—I mean, me.

Five, true to the Nordman money philosophy, I would stash my new paychecks in retirement savings rather than spend it all buying cheap furniture that was no better than the stuff my parents just gave me.

And six, "inheriting" used furniture helped me maintain a frugal lifestyle full of frugal tastes. Of course I could go out to top-of-the line furniture stores to get the very best in custom design. But why would I do that?

DOUG
Lifestyle Choices

Whether or not your young adult pursues a degree right after high school, you still want to find ways for them to manage larger sums of money. You're helping them improve their financial skills.

Maybe they'd want to live at home for another year (in Mom's basement?) during their trade school or their first job. Instead of paying rent you could expect them to maximize their Roth IRA contributions or make their employer's full match on their 401(k) account. Be clear that you're not subsidizing their lifestyle. You're ensuring that they invest retirement contributions now (while they're young) for decades of compounding (when they're...older). Exploiting compound growth at an early age is too important for them to screw up.

Managing adult sums of money is a fantastic teachable moment. You want them to gain proficiency at handling large account balances without delaying their maturity or spoiling them. If they blow your financial support to fund their new luxury lifestyle then your help stops and they're going to learn their own hard adult lessons. (It might be years before you consider gifting them again.) When they apply your mentoring to become money-savvy adults, then they'll meet their goals (like maxing out their Roth IRA contributions).

Your young adults will launch themselves from your basement as soon as they save up a security deposit and find a few roommates to pay most of the rent. Maybe they'll even save up a down payment to buy a home or a duplex and house-hack the extra bedrooms with roommates. Your financial support could jumpstart their entrepreneurial real estate investing career.

Your young adult may think that you've transformed into the best parent ever, but there's a much more pragmatic reason for boosting their skills with larger sums: financial independence.

When frugal adults push for a high savings rate and watch their investments grow to six figures, they develop more confidence in their self-worth. While they're still in their 20s, they begin to shift their mindset to abundance instead of scarcity. They start to realize: "There's opportunity everywhere!" instead of living in fear: "But what if I lose my job?!?" They adopt an internal locus of control instead of feeling victimized by external factors. They set goals like "I can learn more and work hard" instead of feeling helpless: "Inflation will never let me get ahead!"

Ironically, managing larger sums of money (and growing wealth) also helps adults to resist the temptation of sacrificing life energy for more money. Do they really want to commit to an employer's multi-year contract for a big retention bonus? (Think about why an employer is suddenly being so nice.) Do they really need to sign up for all of that overtime? Saving and investing gives your new adults the option of negotiating the bonus ("It's only money and not worth my quality of life") instead of living in fear ("OMG I have to take this money—and its three-year commitment—so that I can pay off my credit cards"). Instead of locking themselves into trading more life for more money, they'll find their own incentives for a better life.

They'll learn that they can boost their income (and their savings rate) by transferring into a different department, or they'll find a new job at a company who'll pay them for their higher value. They may even decide that the best way to control their finances and their time is by running their own business.

As they make their choices, they'll blaze their own trails. As they see their net worth growing from a high savings rate, they'll avoid the lifestyle expansion. They'll keenly understand the value of financial independence, and they'll choose their own exit from the corporate treadmill.

Financial independence gives them choices, and they'll work because they want to—not because they have to.

SUMMARY
The Years After High School

A young adult's first few years after high school—whether they're gap years, or spent in college or trade school can deliver a few harsh life lessons.

As your children flap their wings of independence to fly out of the nest, this could be your last chance to coach them through their financial hazards. They might still make their money mistakes at home with you, or they'll catch up with you weeks later to talk about problems. However you hear from them, this is your opportunity to keep the lines of communication open.

They're trying to build on your values (not challenge them) while developing their own identity. We parents might have our own challenges of keeping an open mind as our former teens work through their transition to adulthood.

This is your new chance to relate to your children as adults, not only as Mommy and Daddy. The good news is that you won't have to live with as much teen drama, angst, and hormones. The other news is that as they launch into the world, you might not live with them as much at all.

CHAPTER GOALS

- Write your own letters to your 18-year-old.
- Establish their own checking account and credit cards.
- Give your young adult incentives to manage their education fund (a semester at a time).
- Encourage young adults to learn entrepreneurial skills by earning money at college.

CHAPTER NINE

Parents of Adults

> **"**
>
> WELCOME TO THE REAL WORLD!
> IT SUCKS. YOU'RE GONNA
> LOVE IT!
>
> MONICA GELLAR
> *FRIENDS*, THE TV SHOW

FINANCIAL TERMS AND CONCEPTS IN THIS CHAPTER

- Embracing frugality while avoiding deprivation.
- Achieving (and maintaining!) a high savings rate.
- Investments and compound growth.

DOUG
A New Relationship With Your Young Adult

In the last chapter we parents mentioned that we wanted our adult daughter to see us as mentors and life coaches, not as "Mom and Dad."

Well, that was a total failure. A few years after college, our daughter married an outstanding son-in-law. Today we have twice as many people calling us "Mom and Dad," and I've never been prouder to hear it.

Fortunately it turns out that we can all do both. We may be Mom and Dad forever, but we're also deep into that mentoring phase.

We started our informal life-coaching seminars right after college. Our daughter had been a very successful steward of her college fund, and we parents still had a healthy collection of CDs set to mature at her graduation. We had promised her profit-sharing, and we started with a big one: $28,000. It was the tax code's annual gifting exclusion limit.

By 2014, we had put the Great Recession behind us, and our investment portfolio had taken off. It was clear that our 4% Safe Withdrawal Rate plans (see Appendix B) were working out very well, and that we'd have enough wealth to leave a legacy for the next generation.

We decided to not only share the profits of the college fund, but to pass on some inheritance while we were all still around to talk about it. $28K is a huge chunk of change to dump on a 21-year-old in the middle of college graduation, but we knew that the military would also be dumping similar sums on her head. This was her chance to enjoy the "Woo-hoo!" of the wealth effect, to feel the emotions and the responsibility, and to make the best decisions she could with the money skills she had learned.

Every parent wants to be confident that they've given their progeny the skills to succeed. However we knew that $28K could also make a perfect down payment on an awesome shiny-new Mustang GT convertible. If our daughter was going to throw away all of her fiscally-responsible habits and give in to temptation, then we'd rather find out now.

It seemed like a fairly safe experiment. We'd seen what she did with her Bank Of Carol 401(k) and her college car purchase. We were pretty sure she'd handle the gifting just fine—and she did.

She used her money as we suggested: maximizing her contributions to her Roth 401(k) and her Roth IRA, and saving even more in her emergency fund and her taxable investment account.

It also showed us an example of "What a parent says" versus "What a teen hears." Carol's interpretation of our parental advice went way beyond what we parents expected, and her extraordinary achievement dramatically accelerated her financial goals.

Ever since our daughter was in middle school she's heard us parents preach, er, I mean, point out the math of financial independence. If you invest 40% of your gross income (a challenging number!) in a high-equity portfolio, then you can reach FI within 20 years.

When our daughter started her Navy career and transferred overseas to her first ship in Rota, Spain, she rented a decent house in a safe neighborhood. She frequently bicycled to the base (Spain has a big bike culture). She shopped frugally on the base and at local markets. She even kept the house fairly cold in wintertime. She spent many hours learning her job and getting qualified, and the ship was underway a lot, so most of her entertainment was dining out with shipmates in foreign ports.

When we visited, we were impressed with her frugal accomplishments. Her work was time-consuming and she didn't have much liberty, but she was clearly enjoying a very fulfilling life. She also felt that she was winning the frugality challenge, especially after hard workdays on the ship. She mentioned that she'd invested her $28K gift as we suggested, but she didn't really go into detail about what she was doing with her military pay.

It took me another year of occasional financial discussions before I realized that she'd not only invested all of her gift, but she'd also gone a step further and invested 40% of her Navy income. Her total savings rate was over 60%. She had jump-started her journey to financial independence by strapping on a booster rocket.

She has not only understood the math of FI—she's going to reach it faster than her parents did!

It became clear that we'd launched a money-savvy adult who wasn't going to boomerang back to our basement.[10] Better yet, she was already compounding her "starter inheritance" money for a much bigger impact than if she'd received our legacy in her 50s.

CAROL
From "Living Like A Monk" To "Living Like An Ensign"

One of the phrases Dad has always said in his writings and advice goes something like "live a frugal life, not a deprived life." Frugality, not deprivation, was always the key. One could argue that the life of a monk (or any other religious equivalent) can be seen as a life of deprivation to the average human. While anyone could handle living like a monk for a few years out of necessity—like to accelerate paying off student debt—after a few years, it could be depression-inducing.

The lowest commissioned officer rank in the U.S. Navy is the rank of a "O-1," named an "Ensign," and also known as a "Second Lieutenant" in the other non-nautical branches of the U.S. military. Today's Ensigns typically earn about $60,000 a year before taxes, which is a great starting salary for college graduates with virtually no work or real-life experience. Once an Ensign has maxed out their Thrift Savings Plan (TSP, the military equivalent of a 401(k)), and their Roth IRA, and paid their taxes (let's say they owe 20% total in taxes to the various levels of American government), they have about $23,000 left annually to pay for shelter, clothing, food, transportation, and "fun money."

---

[10] Carol's Note: It's awfully hard to boomerang back to your parents' basement when...well, they physically don't have a basement! Talk about an impossible option!

Annual earnings: $60,000.

Total income taxes (20% x $60K): $12,000.

401(k) or TSP contribution (in 2019): $19,000.

IRA contribution (in 2019): $6000.

Total retirement savings: $19K + $6K = $25,000

Savings Rate (Retirement only): $25K / $60K = 41.67%

Remainder: $60K - $12K - $19K - $6K = $23,000.

Although that remaining $23,000 looks low, it has several advantages. First, because the Ensign has maxed out their TSP and IRA, they've already saved $25,000 annually before taxes, a savings rate of 41.67% without effort. In addition, they've made a few thousand dollars more in retirement savings thanks to employee-matching contributions by the employer, a built-in function of 401(k) plans. Hawk-eyed financial experts will also note that the Ensign doesn't need $23,000 to cover the above remaining expense categories. Depending on the area's cost of living, the Ensign can spend as little as $18,000 a year (roughly $1,500 a month) by home-cooking meals, using cheap transportation (like a bicycle), sharing streaming and other entertainment services (one of the few "utility bills" that multiple paychecks can pay into), and living with roommates (a form of "house hacking") to drive down housing costs. This means that an Ensign could theoretically save a portion of that $23,000 remaining to build an emergency fund and even start investing. This also means the Ensign is really saving more than

41.67%; if they're saving that ($23,000-$18,000 =) $5,000 they didn't spend on annual living expenses, then their annual savings rate is actually 50%, not just 41.67%.

What happens when the Ensign gets a bonus, or a promotion? The Ensign continues to live like an Ensign for as long as possible. That means that the (now former) Ensign doesn't spend the salary raise (say, $13,000 annually) or bonus (say, $15,000 annually), or create a more affluent lifestyle. Instead, the former Ensign puts that extra money right into savings/investments, and continues living the lifestyle they would've had without the promotion or bonus. As a result, the former Ensign increases their savings from that initial 41.67% or 50% savings rate to something possibly as high as 70%, without having to sacrifice or change their lifestyle or start up a side hustle. With the miracle of compounding interest, the initial thousands in savings will be millions in retirement by the time the Ensign turns 59½ years old and can start to withdraw tax-advantaged funds without penalty.

Again, the concept of living like an Ensign is to promote frugality, not deprivation. If one gets married, it may be time to shed the roommate-shared lifestyle and find a new abode for just the couple. If children come into the picture, the extra mouth(s) to feed and care for may cost more than the Ensign can afford. If the Ensign lifestyle starts to feel like deprivation for your family, it's time to stop living like an O-1, and start spending like an O-2 instead; someone who

> IF THEY'RE SAVING THAT ($23,000–$18,000 =) $5,000 THEY DIDN'T SPEND ON ANNUAL LIVING EXPENSES, THEN THEIR ANNUAL SAVINGS RATE IS ACTUALLY 50%, NOT JUST 41.67%

earns an extra $13,000 a year before taxes. And when living like an O-2 is deprivation for the O-4 and the growing family, start living like an O-3 (an extra $20,000 before taxes), and so on. All throughout, they can continue to maximize their retirement savings for as long as possible, which means they can achieve FI sooner.

Living like an Ensign is purely a choice. But like many financial choices, it's your choice, and it's a pretty powerful one to have. You may find that you enjoy the security that comes with living like an Ensign. You may find a newfound joy in watching your savings account climb to new, unimaginable amounts. You may find a new sense of freedom in not having to take care of extra stuff or unexpected maintenance.

Suze Orman has famously said, "people first, then money, then things." By practicing the "live like an Ensign concept," one will naturally change their lifestyle for the important people in their lives first: their family.

DOUG
Getting Your Young Adult's Investing Off To A Good Start

I'll admit it up front: our daughter accelerated her financial independence because she graduated from college without student debt.

It's tempting to call that a privilege. As a finance author (and a parent) I've become keenly aware of society's obstacles to the success of women and minorities. When your teens finish high school, scholarships and work-study programs might not be enough. We recognize that student debt may be deemed necessary for some career fields. If that happens, then a high savings rate is just as important to paying off debt as it is to building wealth.

If Carol had decided to spend more money on her education (for a masters or medical school) then that would have used up the rest of her college fund (no money left for profit sharing!). Instead of choosing student debt, we would have encouraged work-study, scholarships, or even working for a few years to save up for the advanced degree.

Regardless of your young adult's choices, a high savings rate will still accelerate their journey to financial independence. It's a combination of a frugal lifestyle and the perpetual quest for a higher income— whether that comes from job training, promotions, switching employers, or a new career field.

Financial independence requires investing as well as paying off debt. As a parent, you're much more aware of the impact of compound growth (and the passing years) than your child is. Compounding means that it's important for young adults to invest for FI while they're still paying off their debt. Once your graduate has built up a small emergency fund, they absolutely have to invest as much as they can to earn the employer's match in their 401(k). If they want to pay off their student debt faster than the minimum payments then they should figure out how to earn more, not simply cannibalize their investments. Whether they're promoted at work or start a part-time side hustle, they have to invest a minimum amount for retirement before they throw the "extra" money at debt.

A high savings rate overcomes many other challenges on the way to financial independence. Yet those investments will compound faster with an aggressive asset allocation, even while they'll also be more volatile. Investors can minimize other risks by choosing passively-managed stock index funds with low expense ratios. The only funds necessary, in my opinion, are a total-stock-market index fund and a total-bond-market fund, although they may want to experiment with other funds or even pick individual stocks. The best approach is to limit those experiments to 10% of an asset allocation. It's large enough to move the needle if they turn out to be brilliant investors, and small enough to limit the damage if they're not.

The key to asset allocation is beating inflation while still sleeping comfortably at night. Yet we're humans, and the emotions of behavioral financial psychology will always try to override math and logic. I'd like to think that we could all read and learn enough about investing to become comfortable with volatility. For most beginning investors, though, the best approach is to pick an asset allocation, put the contributions on autopilot through paycheck deductions, and then try to ignore the financial "news." Read books and websites about investing. Listen to financial podcasts and watch videos, but don't watch CNBC.

Your young adult has to learn their tolerances and comfort zones, and you can help them adult in a way which suits them. Young workers should try to allocate at least 70% of their investments to equities, and if their employment income seems reliable then they could go even higher. If they're concerned about unemployment then they can build a larger emergency fund instead of investing more conservatively. The long-term returns of an aggressive asset allocation are worth the short-term volatility. Your experience with volatile markets and recessions can help them build their own experience.

Browse our "Resources" section at the back for more books, websites, podcasts, and videos. Experience is the best way to get comfortable with investing, but education is the next-best way to sleep comfortably at night.

CAROL
Ain't Nobody Got Time For That

My high savings rate was partially born out of my ridiculous lack of time.

When I was a freshman in college, I barely had time to watch TV on a regular basis because I was studying so much. As a new Ensign in the U.S. Navy, assigned to a ship with a reputation as "the workhorse of the fleet," I was working six days a week and barely had enough time to get six hours of sleep a night, even on weekends and holidays. To say "I was busy" was an understatement for my first two years in my naval career. The good news was I was getting paid handsomely (for a recent college grad). I barely had any time to spend my paycheck.

When you barely have time to sleep, all of life's priorities shift. I didn't care what my furniture looked like when I came home; I just wanted to take a shower, eat a quick meal while wearing pajamas, and go to bed. I didn't care what the latest streaming media craze was (I'm looking at you, *Game of Thrones*); I just wanted to get an extra hour of sleep in before I went back to work. I didn't care about the latest fashion trends in clothing and transportation; I just wanted clean, work-appropriate laundry and a reliable bicycle or car to get me to and from the long days.

Although I had little time, I continued to keep up with my bank account balances. I made sure I was paid the right amount each month, that the right auto-transfer was made to my 401(k) and other investment accounts outside my bank, and that all my bills (on credit cards) were paid on time via auto-pay. I then transferred any money leftover to the same mutual fund I was already making a monthly auto-deposit in. As Mr. Money Mustache describes in his famous blog,[11] I was turning my money into my own army of workers that was making me more money. If I was going to work long and hard, then my money was going to work just as long and hard as I was.

When I finally transferred to a new assignment that had somewhat shorter hours and was located on land, my lifestyle barely changed. I didn't go on shopping splurges, or buy new "toys." I did buy a "new" used car, but that was because my old car was finally getting too old.

Although I was still working long hours, I found that I was happy. This happiness didn't come from a fat savings account, or from an accumulation of stuff. The happiness came from peace of mind and security in knowing I could handle the real world. It came from knowing that my early investments were going to earn (pardon the pun) a boatload of compounding interest, and secure my retirement. I realized how much I valued this happiness and security; how much joy it brought me. I resolved to keep saving as much as I could for as long as I could.

The other big revelation was that I was now cemented as a passive investor. At the beginning of my career, before my long hours started, I'd asked my Dad and other family friends about recommended stock market fund allocations, as Dad mentioned earlier. Once I found and signed up for mutual funds with these allocations, I set up an auto-deposit program between my checking account and my mutual fund, and an auto-buy program for buying shares with my deposited cash. While I checked my bank accounts at least once a month, I didn't look at my investment accounts for months at a time. Of course I would always log into the fund every once in a while to ensure everything was humming along; it always was.

---

[11] "Your Money Can Work Harder Than You Can." Mr. Money Mustache, January 30, 2012, www.mrmoneymustache.com/.

Today, my husband is a more active investor than I am. By the time he got into saving and investing—around the time our casual dating turned serious—he was intrigued by the trends of the stock market and its relation to world economies. He enjoys following financial news and doing research. He tweaks his portfolio allocations about once every six months and checks the daily balance changes, while I go years at a time without making adjustments and don't care about the day-to-day economics. Although I had a head start on investing, my husband's smarter investment portfolio is doing as well as mine is.

SUMMARY
When Your Young Adults Leave The Nest

As your young adults leave the nest, their standard of living will change. Help them understand the difference between frugality and deprivation. Frugality is challenging and fulfilling, not a sacrifice. (It feels like winning!) Deprivation is useful for short-term goals but is not sustainable.

A high savings rate will overcome many smaller mistakes. Compounding is hard to perceive in the early years, but after 5-10 years you will see exponential growth. The most important financial decisions to optimize are marriage, buying or renting a home, transportation, and food. Keep cutting out the waste in your lives but don't obsess over the small mistakes.

We love our families, but we parents would NOT have dipped into our retirement funds to pay for education. There are no scholarships for retirement, and we parents were not interested in working longer! More importantly, young adults do not want to jeopardize their parents' financial security or have to support them when they're older.

You can help your adult children avoid a lot of family stress by talking with them about your own estate plan. Don't just write it down and put it in the "Emergency" folder. Share your thoughts, have a family discussion, and help them understand how to implement it. It's also a great way to continue your own mentoring and coaching through leading by example.

CHAPTER GOALS

- Practice frugality (track spending, minimize waste). Avoid deprivation.
- Achieve and maintain a high savings rate.
- Choose an asset allocation and leave it in the market as long as possible.

CHAPTER TEN

Generational Wealth and Estate Planning

> ## 66
>
> I'LL GIVE MY CHILDREN ENOUGH MONEY
> SO THAT THEY FEEL THEY COULD DO
> ANYTHING, BUT NOT SO MUCH THAT THEY
> COULD DO NOTHING.
>
> WARREN BUFFETT

FINANCIAL TERMS AND CONCEPTS
IN THIS CHAPTER

**FINANCIAL TERMS AND CONCEPTS
IN THIS CHAPTER**

- Estate planning.
- Gifting and inheritances.
- Mentoring and coaching your next generation
  for financial independence.

DOUG
Managing Your Money While You're Still Around To Talk About It

When you're teaching your family to manage money, it's not only about the next generation—it's about you. Your kids have to confidently handle their own money because one day they may have to manage your money for you. You also want them to feel secure in their fiduciary responsibilities without being tempted to help themselves to someone else's assets.

Our daughter was a tough kid to raise, which may be one reason that she has no siblings. We parents both have siblings, and we're very personally familiar with sibling rivalry. However much we fought with our brothers when we were younger, today (many years later) we've managed to set aside our differences and work together.

We can't help you mediate the inevitable sibling rivalries, but we're pretty sure that more family communication means less confusion. The more you manage the expectations of your kids, and the more you tell your young adults about your assets, the more ready they'll be to step up if the time comes.

I learned this the hard way when my father developed dementia. He never discussed his finances with us. ("I'm fine, boys!") He never even kept an "In Case Of Emergency" folder listing his accounts and assets, let alone set up a power of attorney for us. As Alzheimer's took his cognition, the word "No" became the easiest answer in his vocabulary. Eighteen months later when he was inevitably unable to live independently, I spent hours searching for a list of his accounts and passwords. I not only managed his finances for another six years (without any guidance from him) but I was perpetually searching for other wayward assets.

It took over six months just to file my father's claim on his long-term care insurance policy. (It also cost nearly $4,000 for the neuropsychological exams to prove what we already knew about his Alzheimer's.) It took 10 months (and over $6,000 in lawyer bills) to obtain legal permission to manage Dad's assets. By the time the courts appointed my brother and me as our father's guardian and conservator, we had spent nearly $25,000 of our money on Dad's care.

We reimbursed ourselves from his accounts, but we spent the next six years filing more legal reports. We not only took care of Dad, but we had to keep detailed track of Dad's accounts and report every penny of income and expenses to the probate court. Along with all of the stress of caring for an elder, we had the additional stress of working with the court while worrying that we could be "fired" at any time.

Thankfully, my brother and I agreed on what had to be done, and we made a good team. I can only imagine how much it would have cost to take care of Dad if we sons lacked financial skills or if sibling rivalry had been an issue.

Your financial management can prepare your children to step up if you need help, and you can also make sure that they understand your plans and needs. As you raise your family (and deal with the inevitable sibling rivalry), you'll encourage teamwork. You'll avoid putting the kids in situations where they feel obligated to compete with each other, even if it's the annual gathering for the holiday meal. You'll spend lots of time setting the family rules and getting everyone to understand why you make your decisions.

You can give each of your kids the same allowance (in age-appropriate amounts) and the same financial incentives. ("Everyone has to finish their chores before they can do a job for money.") You can try to equalize the gifts at birthdays and holidays. You can even try to balance the time that you spend with your kids, although you'll know that some of them need more of your time than others.

It's the same situation with college funds, adult gifting, and even inheritances.

Maybe each of your children gets the same amount of money for college, whether they're studying engineering or liberal arts. They'd have the same assets to spend at a community college or an Ivy League school—assuming that they even want to go to college. Does one sibling get extra money for medical school or an MBA? What if one of them wants to take a gap year, or even drop out of college to start a business?

My only advice is to open the family's financial books a little, explain how much money is in the college fund, and give them the same amounts to work with. They'll figure out the schools, majors, and scholarships. They'll make their own plans for a trade career, a gap year, or a law degree.

By the time they're in their 20s, you'll have a good idea of their ability to handle larger amounts of money. You'll know who's a saver, a spendthrift, or an investor. You'll still help them to learn how to handle their adult incomes and overcome their weaknesses.

This is also the time to start discussing your retirement finances, and to help them learn how you plan to manage your money for the rest of your life. Believe me, they don't want to worry about how you'll support yourself on your investments and whether they'll have to take care of you. You don't want them to be surprised someday when they realize how much money you have (or how little) and how you've handled it.

CAROL
"The Big Number"

"Mom, Dad, how much money do you have?"

I don't remember how young I was when I first asked the question. But I know that I did ask the question at some point in elementary school, when it (finally) occured to me that Mom and Dad might actually be...wealthy. Even before my parents retired from the workforce, I realized that our family was doing better than families that were homeless, but not as well as other families who were living in mansions on beach-front properties. We certainly weren't on the path to being as rich as Warren Buffet's family or the Gates' computer fortune, but we weren't poor either.

At least, I didn't think we were rich...or poor...

Mom and Dad's initial answer is disappointing to most kids: "We have enough." What does "enough" actually mean? Are we secretly rich and you're not telling me? Are we secretly poor and you're not telling me? How much is "rich" and how much is "poor" anyway?

The discussion that followed Mom and Dad's answer was incredibly important. In it, they gave me *qualitative* measures to their wealth; they would have enough to send me to college, and to keep their house for the rest of their lives. They had enough to stop working in a few years, and spend some time in retirement traveling all over the world. They didn't see a need to go out and buy a yacht or a top-of-the-line sports car. They would still love me no matter what their financial situation was. And someday, I would be told "the big number"—the total value of all of their assets.

Throughout my middle school, high school, and college years, the concept of "the big number" was given out slowly with more and more details. When my grandfather entered a nursing home, Mom and Dad explained that "the big number" was big enough to support both Mom and Dad being in a nursing home for a decade or longer. When Mom and Dad lived in my house in Spain for a couple of months, they explained that they could've rented a local house or apartment in town with the "big number." But what was the point in doing that when I welcomed them to stay whenever and however long they liked?[12]

Mom and Dad finally told me the big number when it was clear I was a successful adult in a successful career of my own. Now that I finally knew the exact amount, I was not surprised. Mom and Dad were as rich as I expected them to be for spending 20 years in the workforce, in professional jobs paying professional salaries. The big

---

[12] I should also point out that my parents helped me out when they visited. They didn't pull the "we let you stay under our roof for 17 years so we should stay at your place" card. Instead, they would take care of any list of chores or repairs I needed around the house. They would do the "deep cleaning" of my place, hang pictures, make grocery runs, or make little repairs or shopping errands I never got around to. Mom's Spanish is much better than mine, so she was able to tackle more complex topics with my landlady, like replacing the kitchen oven or asking where I could hang pictures. It was these little things they did that meant a lot to me, and I always welcomed them back.

number would actually sustain them in a nursing home for much longer than I imagined. I was never worried, nor would I need to start worrying, about how they would financially support themselves in their retirement. Finding out the big number was not dramatic, not earth shattering, and really...uneventful.

But as my mother is famous for saying after an exciting military career, "boring is good."

DOUG
Doing Your Estate Planning With Your Adult Children

When my father passed away from Alzheimer's, I handled his estate. I learned (by experience) how financial corporations and insurance companies distribute the assets of a loved one, and how their rules protect both the estate and the heirs. Once again I wish I'd been able to talk with him about his beneficiary choices and his estate plan.

I also inherited a meaningful sum of money at age 57, when I was already financially independent and had enjoyed 16 years of retirement. I'd hoped that my father would spend his money on himself (or choose to give even more of it to charity), yet admittedly he lived over 20 years of his own FI doing the things he wanted to do. As I reflect on our lifestyles I know that he felt he had more money than he needed.

My share of my inheritance from my father is enough to self-insure myself for my long-term care. It's sitting in a personal (taxable) account in a total stock market index fund with very low expense ratios. It's volatile, but I hope it won't be touched for (at least!) two more decades. It's an aggressive asset allocation, and it should grow faster than inflation. Better yet, it'll pay for my long-term care without forcing my caregiver to deal with the stress of arguing with an insurance company.

Best of all, an inheritance is an incredible teachable moment for a young adult to learn to manage six figures of money.

After I finished distributing my father's assets (and filing all the income-tax forms), my spouse and I took another hard look at our own estate planning. Our daughter was in her mid-20s by then, and she had been only 18 years old when my spouse and I had last updated our wills.

She already knew how we wanted her to take care of our estates after we pass away. Yet if we parents become disabled, we want her to be able to take care of us without worrying about money or bureaucracy.

Our research led us to a long series of discussions about account beneficiary designations like "Transfer On Death" and "Payable On Death." Many states even offer a real estate "Transfer On Death Deed." These tools are all very useful, but they only kick in when... we're dead.

But what if we're disabled?

After more research and many hours with lawyers, we added durable powers of attorney and a revocable living trust to our estate plan. All of the paperwork cost just under $6,000. (That's much less money—and far less time—than petitioning the probate court for my father's conservatorship.) Now if my spouse and I are suddenly disabled, our daughter has the legal authority to immediately tap the inherited funds from my father without any delays or bureaucracy. We also made her a co-trustee of our revocable living trust, so she has the legal authority to manage all of our assets. She's still required by the trust (and by state law) to act as our fiduciary, but she can make decisions in our best interest without court oversight or expensive legal proceedings.

Revocable living trusts are also very effective tools for avoiding the cost of estate probate and for controlling the distribution of inheritances. The co-trustees (and successor trustees) can make decisions for disabled adults, spendthrifts, and minors. Trusts can easily be designed to protect the grantors (my spouse and me) rather than to make it easier for our trustees to care for us.

We've placed a tremendous amount of trust and faith in our daughter. We're confident that she can handle it—the preceding parts of this book show how much work we've put into her financial literacy and her proficiency at managing large sums of money.

My spouse and I also understand that our daughter could certainly abuse our trust and faith by using our assets for her own benefit. In the extremely unlikely event that it happens, we parents still have our Social Security and our military pensions to support our care. No matter how much we may mess up our estate planning, the next month will bring a new deposit to our checking accounts.

More importantly, we've talked about our plans with Carol while we're all still around to ask questions and offer other ideas. We'll continue to update our wishes with letters and emails that she can consult when she's making choices on our behalf. We've made it as easy as possible for her to take care of us if the time comes, and she has the skills to manage our estate for us as well as for herself.

CAROL
The Estate Tax Plan

Mom and Dad don't complain about taxes. Just as they were happy to serve their country, they're happy to pay their taxes to it as well.

Maybe it has to do with the fact that they're retired veterans. Maybe it has to do with the fact that we're all descendants of immigrants, and our family history is full of memorable stories that illustrate just how much better life in America is. Surely we can afford to pay 20% of our income back to the very country that will continue to make this lifestyle possible.

On the other hand, they don't see any reason to pay estate taxes. It just doesn't make sense to our family why the transfer of a substantial estate—money that has already been earned and taxed over a lifetime—is taxed again as it passes to a new set of hands. There's got to be a better way to preserve a lifetime's wealth for future generations.

The extreme way to NOT pay estate taxes is to die dead broke. But that in itself is a risky gamble, as many elderly Americans need that money to pay for retirement homes, hospitals, and even hospice care as the end of their lives approaches. You just can't assume that any remaining assets—a classic car, the family home, heirloom jewelry—will cover the expenses. So how can one ensure an estate is passed on without (accidentally) squandering it and without paying estate taxes?

The answer: start giving your wealth to your children as soon as they're legal adults, but only if you want to.

Today's federal laws allow each parent to gift up to $15,000 to each (adult) child annually without paying taxes. That means each kid can receive up to $30,000 a year from Mom *and* Dad combined in tax-free gifting. In a family with multiple kids (and grandkids!) it's easy to see how annual gifting can help draw down an estate to below the estate tax threshold (or as low as $0). Some states have an estate tax threshold as low as $1 million, while the federal estate tax threshold is a little over $11 million.

The other big advantage to gifting (grand)kids is *time*. If a kid receives gifted money from their (grand)parents at a young age, the wisest thing the kid could do is turn around and immediately invest that gift in an aggressive stock portfolio or something like a 529 account. The gift that was nurtured in the (grand)parents' lifetime will continue to grow over a (grand)kid's lifetime; imagine how much a dollar grows over *two or three lifetimes* of investing and compounding interest. Giving a kid a tax-free gift in their 20s, versus a kid inheriting a taxed estate in their 50s or later, is much cheaper tax-wise and more profitable dividend-wise to perpetuate the "family fortune."

Gifting can come in many forms. Besides cash, one can also gift stocks, portfolios, 529 accounts, collectibles, and other possessions totalling up to $15,000 per parent annually. Gifting stocks as-is, instead of liquidating the stocks to cash, avoids paying capital gains tax on the gift, while ensuring your kids still profit from the dividends. Your kids will have to pay capital gains taxes when/if they liquidate the stocks, but that's another transaction for another time.

So where does the gifted money come from? We Nordmans recommend starting with your family's profit-sharing program— the 529 accounts leftover from college, the money saved on textbooks, and whatever else hasn't been paid out of the program. After all, your kid already worked to save the family all that money; if the remaining lump sum is large, it makes sense to pay out their share via annual gifting. From there you can move on to the next most logical thing to gift your kids, which is whatever you think is the next best thing to gift.

We Nordmans also recommend changing your family's internal financial structure. Remember the Bank of Carol that was founded to help a kid like me understand money basics? Well, I'd grown up into a mature adult, and I'd outgrown the basics offered by the Bank of

Carol as well. Instead of totally shutting its doors on me, the Bank of Carol morphed into what we Nordmans now call the "M&D Financial Coaching Foundation"—not a real foundation, but it's a pseudo structure (like the Bank of Carol was) offering Mom and Dad's (M&D) free services and advice related to the more "advanced" topics like taxes, account conversions, charitable giving, advanced investment techniques, estate planning, and a plethora of other money topics that kids and adults alike have yet to master. Many of the topics in the M&D Foundation are intended for later years, when grown kids have flown the nest, settled into a career and a new life, and are ready to reach back to M&D to discuss estates, (grand)kids, and more.

DOUG
"Where Does All Of This Money Come From?!?"

By now you may be wondering how any parent could find the money to gift their children. I can assure you that my spouse and I are not related to Warren Buffett or Bill Gates. (Seriously, we've checked.) You might also be thinking, "Sure, I'd have money left over for gifting if I only had one kid!" You could be right about that.

All of this wealth came from making choices and then letting compound growth do the rest. My spouse and I earned our college scholarships (at military service academies) and then worked long hours at our careers for over 20 years. Our annual incomes only reached six figures in 2000, and we stopped working for money soon after that.

Our high savings rate came from persistently optimizing our spending. If we felt that we were wasting money, we tried to cut it out by doing it ourselves or finding a way to do without it. (We were frugal, but we avoided deprivation and lived a good quality of life.) Whenever we cut an expense, we invested the savings. We made plenty of mistakes along the way, especially with buying houses and with paying high expense ratios in our investment funds. However our high savings rate overcame all of those mistakes.

The compounding continued after we retired. The success rate of the 4% Safe Withdrawal Rate gives you options for building wealth after financial independence. Despite two nasty recessions and bear markets, our fulfilling lifestyle let our wealth continue to grow faster than inflation.

We remember starting our adult lives as broke college students. We were tired of that life, and our attitudes led to better choices. When you start making your own smart money choices, your compound growth will start working for you too. That growth is hard to detect at first, but the growth of the first decade will tremendously accelerate your net worth during the second decade.

The financial independence movement didn't exist when we started our careers in 1982, yet we achieved our FI within 20 years. Today, the math and the tools are widely accepted and available all over the Internet. When you apply those tools to your own smart choices, your net worth will accelerate and you'll reach your own FI.

That's where the gifting money comes from.

SUMMARY
Protecting And Passing Wealth To The Next Generation

Estate planning is built on trust and open communication between generations.

You can help your adult children avoid tremendous family stress by talking with them about your own estate plan and exploring some "what if" scenarios.

Don't just write it down and put it in the "Emergency" folder. Share your thoughts, have a family discussion, and help them understand how to implement it. It's also a great way to continue your own mentoring and coaching through leading by example.

CHAPTER GOALS

- Discuss your estate planning with your heirs so that they know your intentions.
- Consider gifting as part of practicing the management of large sums.
- Mentor and coach your young adults while you're still around to talk about money.

Epilogue

CAROL
Team Pittner's Choice

At the time of this writing, my husband K.J. and I are in our late twenties, have been married for nearly four years, and we're welcoming our first child into the world. After graduating from college[13] in the same year, we both spent the first five years after college on Active Duty in the U.S. Navy. As I write this book, I've switched from "full time" Active Duty to "part time" Reserves, while K.J. has remained on Active Duty. The family also moved to a higher cost of living area, which meant the military allowances K.J. earns (as the Active Duty member) also increased. This means that, overall, our household income dropped from roughly $160,000 last year to roughly $100,000 this year.

Having me switch from Active Duty to Reserves was a much-needed change and a very important choice for us. K.J. thoroughly enjoys his job and the long hours it requires, while I felt I'd spent one day too many coming home demoralized, after dark, or from work on the weekend... and for what? At one point my office (a ship) re-located 20 miles away from where we lived, across a bridge-tunnel that prohibited bicycling, which meant I now spent an additional 1-2 hours commuting *by car* each day and added a lot of miles to the odometer. Because the new location had very limited and unguarded parking, I found myself waking up at 0415 (!) every morning to "beat the rush" and get a parking spot before work started at 0800. My burnout was obvious at home, and I found myself increasingly repressing my discontent at work.

---

[13] My Mom, Dad, and husband all graduated from the United States Naval Academy, and would strongly argue that it's "not college." However, since we all earned a Bachelors' of Science degree upon graduation, we're all still technically college graduates. It's a Service Academy thing.

Although my part-time status led to a big income cut, we also took a big expense cut. When we were both working full time, we found ourselves "throwing money at problems" so that we could save time instead. This meant we drove two cars instead of bicycling or riding a bus to and from work, and spent our evenings crashed on the couch watching yet another new movie we purchased while eating just-delivered take-out. When we considered adding kids into the picture, we shuddered at the huge cost of daycare, as well as the years-long waiting lists just to get *in* to daycare, and our already dwindling free time thanks to our increased responsibilities at work. Our family, our health, our time, and our happiness have to come first.

Now that I'm the Reservist and homemaker/writer, we're living a happier and healthier lifestyle. I have time to cook, clean, take care of the house, take care of the kid(s) at home, and even write this book with Dad through multiple time zones. Whenever an obstacle arises—K.J. is delayed at work, something breaks in the house, or something is wrong with the kids—I'm there to handle it, and my presence makes the problem cheaper and easier to solve. Since I can work virtually wherever and (almost) whenever, we reside closer to K.J.'s office, which means he can bicycle to work again and even get a workout in at his base's gym. Since neither one of us needs a car regularly, we cut down to one fuel-efficient and family-friendly car; we instantly cut our gas, insurance, and maintenance costs, as well as the time we spent commuting. That means our car costs are only 40% of what they used to be. It made me happier knowing that our car wasn't parked in a lot or parking garage all day, possibly being broken into and quickly depreciating in value the whole while.

My small annual income hovers around $10,000, and makes it hard to totally maximize my annual retirement savings, but we can afford that change since we are saving money in other areas. We're still maxing out my husband's retirement accounts, squirrelling away nearly all of my meager paychecks into my retirement accounts, and even sending a little money to our investment accounts.

I'm also incredibly thankful I saved as much as I did while I was still on Active Duty. Even though I can't maximize my annual retirement savings now, the money saved in my Roth IRA and TSP over the past five years will continue to grow, even though my income took a nosedive.

There is still one lingering question: when will we reach financial independence? We've technically already achieved FI at age 27—our "big number" is just big enough for our frugal lifestyle, even with our newest family member(s). That being said, K.J. and I still haven't done everything we want to do in the military, nor have we found the neighborhood we want to settle down in as we raise our children. Our portfolio isn't aligned for full-fledged retirement, either, because we aren't quite ready to retire (yet). So for now, we plan on doing the military thing for at least another handful of years, making some adjustments to our asset allocation, and seeing where our future military assignments take us.

Most importantly, we get to spend more time together, and that's something we find priceless.

APPENDIX A

The Money-Savvy Family's "Kid 401(k)"

We describe the Kid 401(k) in Chapter 5. This table shows how the compounding works for a series of deposits which grow at 1% per month (12% per year). You can copy this table for your family, or you can use a compound-interest calculator to determine your own growth of a series of deposits.

The table starts at a kid's 8th birthday and assumes that they contribute $3/week of their allowance during a 52-week year. Parents match that contribution at $4.16/week, and the money compounds monthly.

All of the numbers on the table reflect annual totals at the beginning of each year. The child celebrates their 8th birthday with a zero balance and starts making the contributions. At the end of the first year, their contributions (and parental matching) reach $372. Compounding begins slowly at just $25 that first year, but it accelerates during the following years.

By their 16th birthday, the steady contributions have grown to just over $5000.

Here are the table's inputs:

- 12% annual percentage yield (compounded at 1% per month).
- Kid's contribution of $13/month ($3 per weekly allowance).
- Parental match of $18/month (just over $4/week).
- Each year's total contributions are ($13 + 18) x 12 = $372.

AGE	YEAR DEPOSITS	TOTAL DEPOSITS	TOTAL INTEREST	BALANCE
8	0	0	0	0
9	$372.00	$372.00	$25.09	$397.09
10	$372.00	$744.00	$100.54	$844.54
11	$372.00	$1,116.00	$232.74	$1,348.74
12	$372.00	$1,488.00	$428.88	$1,916.88
13	$372.00	$1,860.00	$697.08	$2,557.08
14	$372.00	$2,232.00	$1,046.47	$3,278.47
15	$372.00	$2,604.00	$1,487.35	$4,091.35
16	$372.00	$2,976.00	$2,031.32	$5,007.32

APPENDIX B

The 4% Safe Withdrawal Rate

We're not going to talk about the details of reaching financial independence. The FI research and analysis is all over the Internet, and our Resources section can send you down that rabbit hole.

But we will share the best tip: the 4% Safe Withdrawal Rate (SWR).

It has two parts:

1) You're financially independent when your assets reach 25 times the amount of your annual spending (4% is 1/25). This is the point where you can stop relying on paychecks.

2) You can start your FI life by withdrawing 4% of the value of your assets at the beginning of your first year. Every year afterward you can raise that withdrawal by the inflation rate.

The 4% SWR computer simulations show enough statistical resilience for your investments to survive at least 30 years, although there are a few failures. Your investments may last for at least 60 years, although there's not enough stock-market data to be statistically confident in the results.

Humans don't focus on the success rate. We're optimized to obsess over the failures.

Here are the solutions for the failures, even though a failure is unlikely.

The 4% SWR research does not include Social Security income or other annuities (like a pension). Your investments will almost certainly make it to your minimum age for Social Security, and then that inflation-adjusted annuity will let your portfolio recover. For some Americans, Social Security may be all the longevity insurance that you'll ever need.

The 4% SWR research assumes that spending rises every year with inflation because it's easier to program those computer simulations, yet humans are not SWR robots. We can use variable spending to boost our investment portfolio's survival.

When a recession hits, you'll delay big spending (like a fantasy vacation or a replacement vehicle) and maybe even cut back (temporarily) on your monthly entertainment spending. You may be worried, but you won't face deprivation.

When the economy is booming your investments will grow much faster than inflation or your spending—and that growth will rebuild your portfolio's survivability margin for the next recession.

Even if there's a recession (or two) during your first decade of FI, then during the second decade your investments will probably still compound fast enough to reduce your actual withdrawal rate (your latest annual expenses divided by your latest portfolio value) to less than 4%.

If a full-on Great Depression repeats itself, then variable spending will help your portfolio survive. (Variable spending was only necessary for a tiny part of the Great Depression.) If a new depression is even worse, then your variable spending will ease the pressure of the annual withdrawals. You don't even need to start variable spending until after the first year or two of the economic catastrophe. You'll see the problem coming from a long way off, and you'll only need to cut back a little to avoid failure.

You could even get a part-time job, and at the 4% SWR you might only need to work for 10 hours per week to earn about $10,000 per year. You might only need it for 6-12 months. Depressions have very high unemployment, but those part-time jobs are everywhere because employers can't pay full-time salaries while (unemployed) workers want full-time jobs.

But what if you reached FI and worked for another year or two to reduce your withdrawal rate below the 4% SWR? That seems pretty easy, right?

This logic trap is so widespread that it has a diagnosis: the Just One More Year (JOMY) Syndrome.

JOMY Syndrome looks great, because the 4% SWR is already good enough and a small annuity can insure that plan against failure. JOMY only piles on more assets and guarantees that you'll die with even more money. A decade after you start your FI life, you'll realize that you wasted a year of your life to delay that decade. Was it worth it?

More importantly, is it worth working one more year to reduce your scarcity stress and to sleep better at night? Will you feel better despite having more work stress, spending less time with your family, and trading life energy for excess money?

Only you can answer that behavioral economics question. The math and the 4% SWR research says that you're wasting your time.

Starting with the 4% SWR, perhaps with a little annuity income and variable spending, your investments will last for the rest of your life.

You'll also have plenty of money to pass to the next generation. You could hand over that legacy in a lump sum, or you could spread it out a little at a time over many years.

That's how you can help your money-savvy family reach financial independence.

That's why we wrote this book.

RESOURCES

Books, Websites, Podcasts, and Videos

The Books We Used While Raising Carol

Brain, Marshall. 1997. *The Teenager's Guide to the Real World.* Raleigh, NC: BYG Publishing.

Dacyczyn, Amy. 1999. *The Tightwad Gazette: Promoting Thrift as a Viable Alternative Lifestyle.* New York: Villard Press.

Owen, David. 2004. *First National Bank of Dad: The Best Way to Teach Kids about Money.* Darby, PA: Diane Publishing Co.

Savage, Marjorie. 2009. *You're on Your Own (but I'm Here If You Need Me): Mentoring Your Child during the College Years.* New York: Touchstone (Simon & Schuster).

Schwartz, David M., and Steven Kellogg. 1994. *If You Made a Million.* Video/Audio Book. Danbury, CT: Weston Woods Studios.

Vanderkam, Laura. 2012. *All the Money in the World: What the Happiest People Know about Wealth.* New York: Portfolio/Penguin.

Wyatt, Elaine, and Stan Hinden. 1999. *The Money Book and Hideaway Bank: a Smart Kid's Guide to Savvy Saving and Spending.* Toronto, CAN: Somerville House.

Books Recommended By Teen And Adult Carol

Clason, George, and Frederick Van Rensselaer Dey. 2018. *The Richest Man In Babylon: with The Magic Story.* San Diego, CA: Dauphin Publications. (Note: this book has multiple editions. Check your public library.)

Huddleston, Cameron. 2019. *Mom and Dad, We Need to Talk: How to Have Essential Conversations with Your Parents about Their Finances.* Hoboken, NJ: John Wiley & Sons.

Kondō, Marie. 2014. *The Life-Changing Magic of Tidying up: The Japanese Art of Decluttering and Organizing.* New York: Ten Speed Press (Crown Publishing Group).

Nordman, Doug. 2011. *The Military Guide to Financial Independence & Retirement.* Manassas, VA: Impact Publications. (Note: Carol specifically requested that we include this book. Absolutely check your local public library or military base library to read it for free!)

Ramsey, Dave. 2007. *The Total Money Makeover.* Nashville, TN: Thomas Nelson, Inc.

Stanley, Thomas J. 1996. *The Millionaire Next Door: The Surprising Secrets of America's Wealthy.* New York: Pocket Books.

Carol also recommends the Hoopla digital library app, especially for audiobooks. She listened to Marie Kondo's and Dave Ramsey's books during her commutes.

Websites

Concannon, Kevin. 2014. "USDA Cost of Raising a Child Calculator." U.S. Department of Agriculture. https://www.usda.gov/media/blog/2017/01/13/cost-raising-child/.

Blogs

Adeney, Peter. 2012. Mr. Money Mustache. www.mrmoneymustache. com/.

Nordman, Doug. 2010. "About The Military Guide - The Book And The Blog." The Military Guide. https://the-military-guide.com/about/.

Podcasts

Jensen, Mindy, and Scott Trench. 2018. "BiggerPockets Money Show: Investing & Wealth Building." BiggerPockets. www.biggerpockets. com/moneyshow.

Videos

Orman, Suze. 2016. "Can I Afford It?" Suze Orman's Official Channel. https://www.youtube.com/playlist?list=PL2Wlw4brxKIuswH32jxfhc8h_ yXz6c9Zu.

Carol

THANK YOU TO MY SPOUSE, MY FAMILY, OUR PUBLISHERS, AND EVERYONE ELSE WHO BOTHERED TO EITHER TALK WITH US OR READ OUR WORK! ANOTHER THANK YOU GOES OUT TO CHRISTOPHER SATO, MY TWO-YEAR HIGH SCHOOL ENGLISH TEACHER, WHO TRULY TAUGHT ME HOW TO DEVELOP MY OWN VOICE IN WRITING.

Doug

BOOKS STILL DON'T WRITE THEMSELVES, EVEN WHEN YOU SUCKER YOUR FAMILY INTO DICTATING THE WORDS INTO YOUR KEYBOARD.

MY DEEPEST THANKS TO THE WHOLE NEW CROP OF BETA READERS. WITHOUT YOU, I'D JUST BE WEARING OUT KEYBOARDS AND ANNOYING THE REST OF MY HOUSEHOLD.

AND YES, I'M DELIVERING A FEW COPIES OF THIS BOOK TO MR. SATO—ALONG WITH OUR ETERNAL PARENTAL GRATITUDE.

CPSIA information can be obtained
at www.ICGtesting.com
Printed in the USA
BVHW070253040920
588089BV00002B/161